i loved you
the moment
i saw you

Peter Black

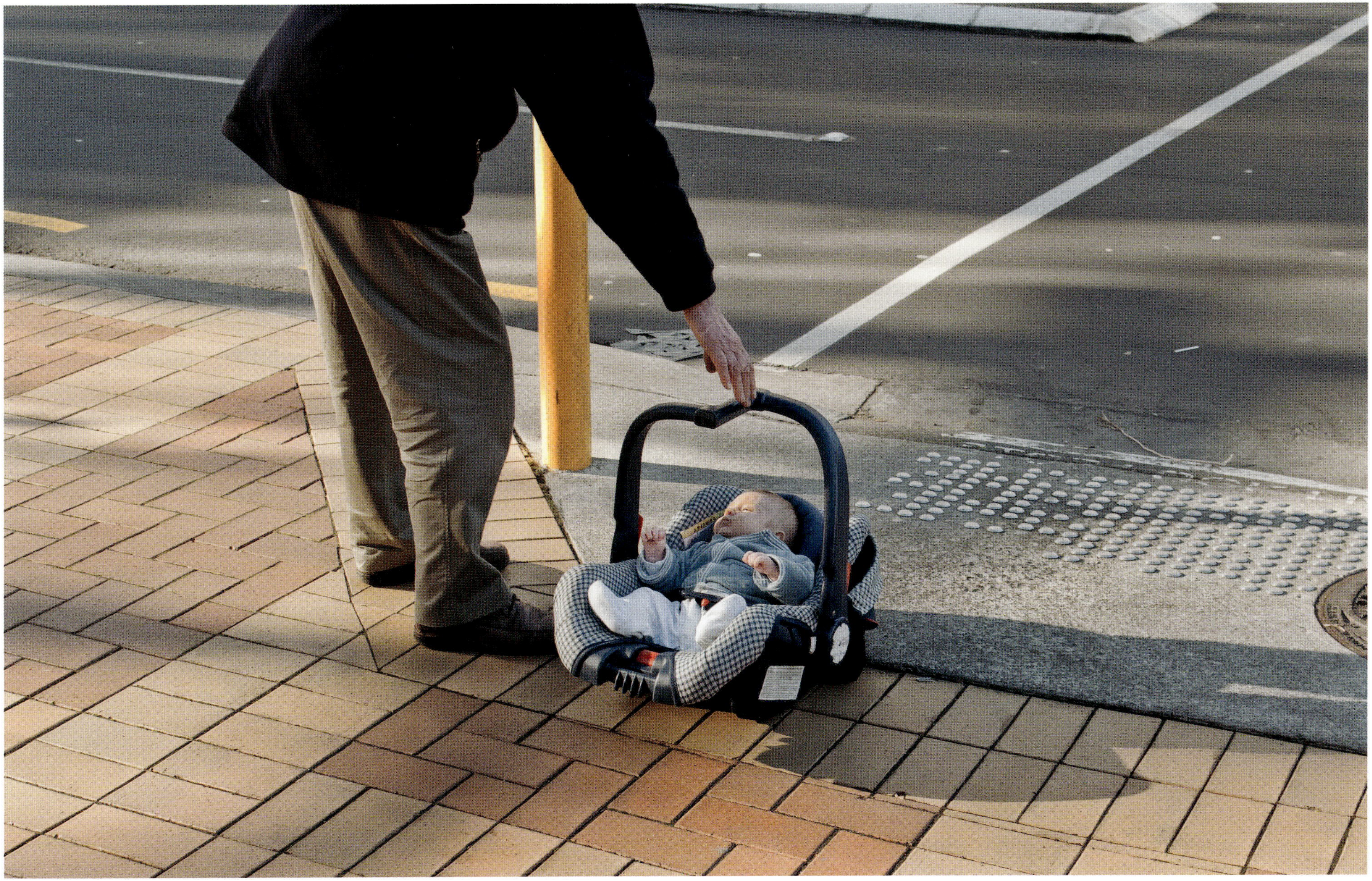

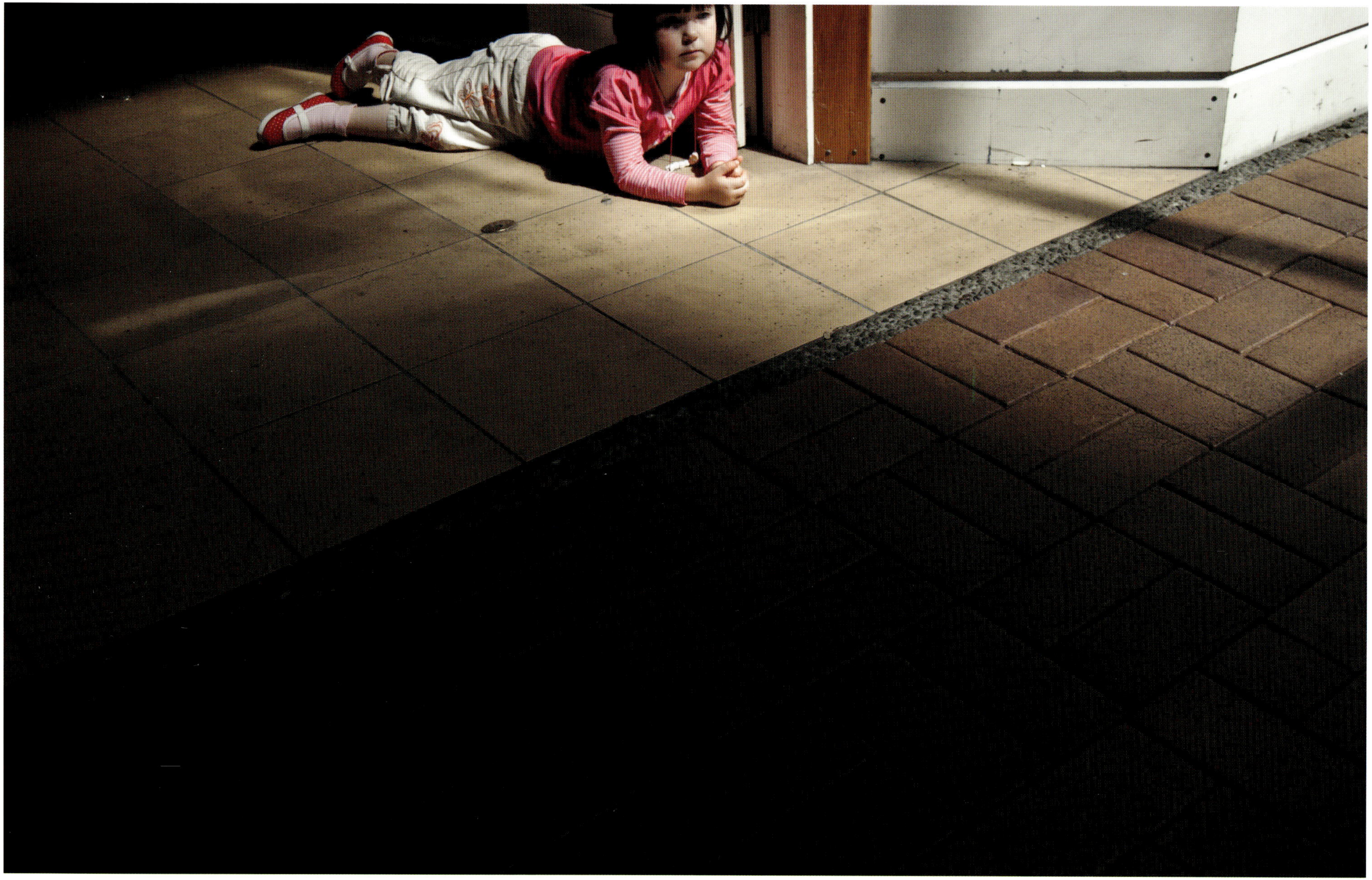

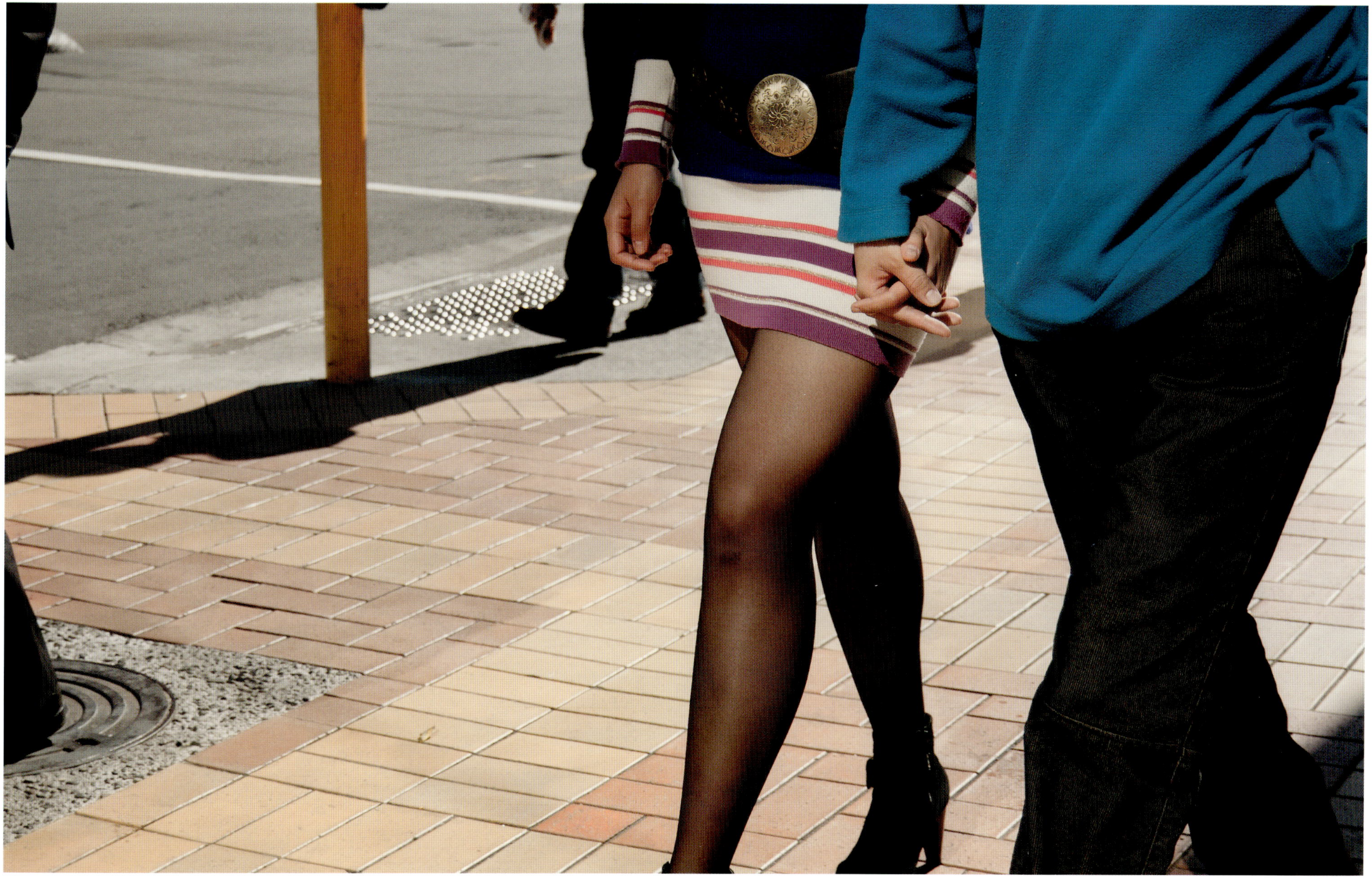

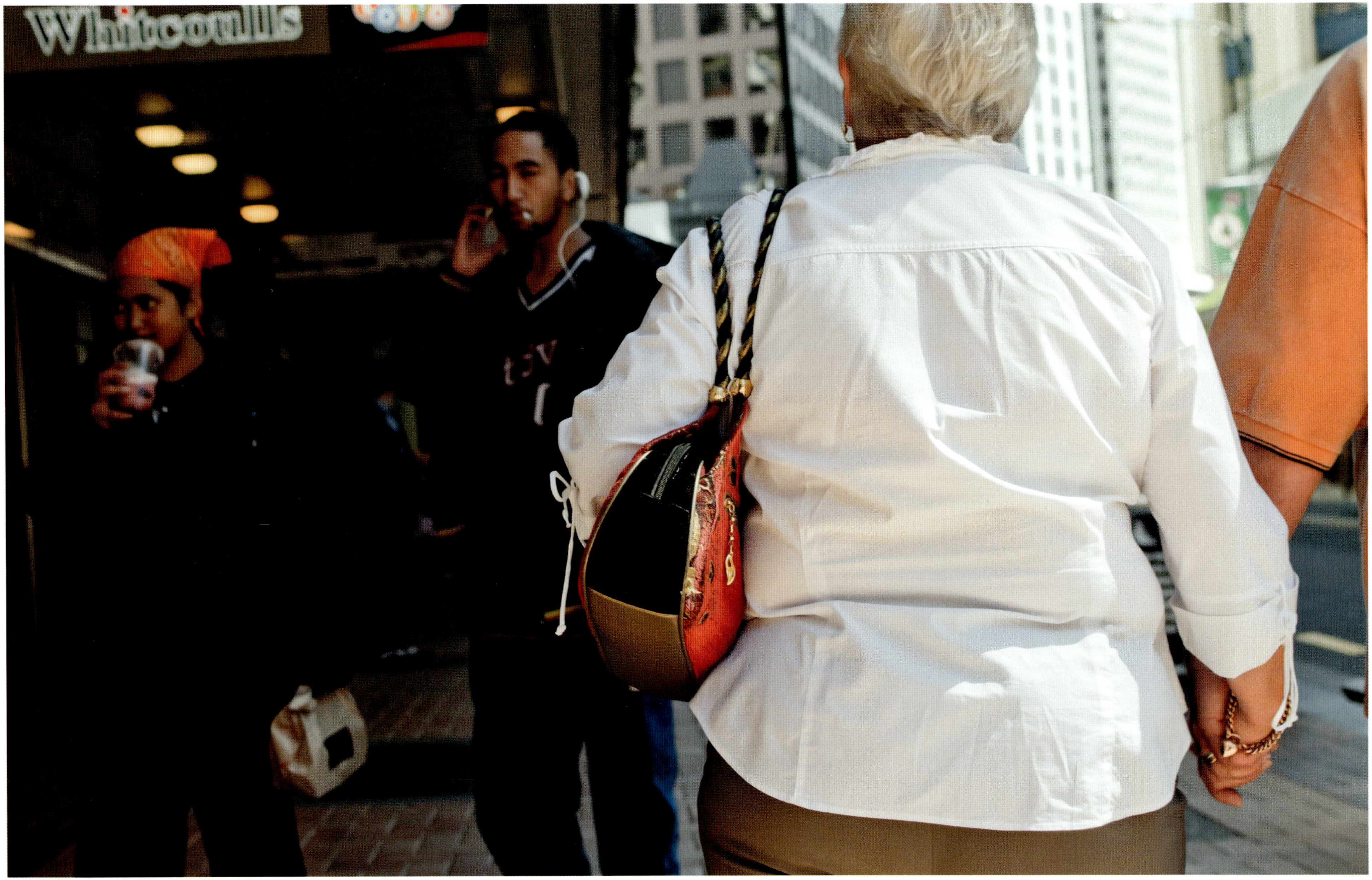
Whitcoulls

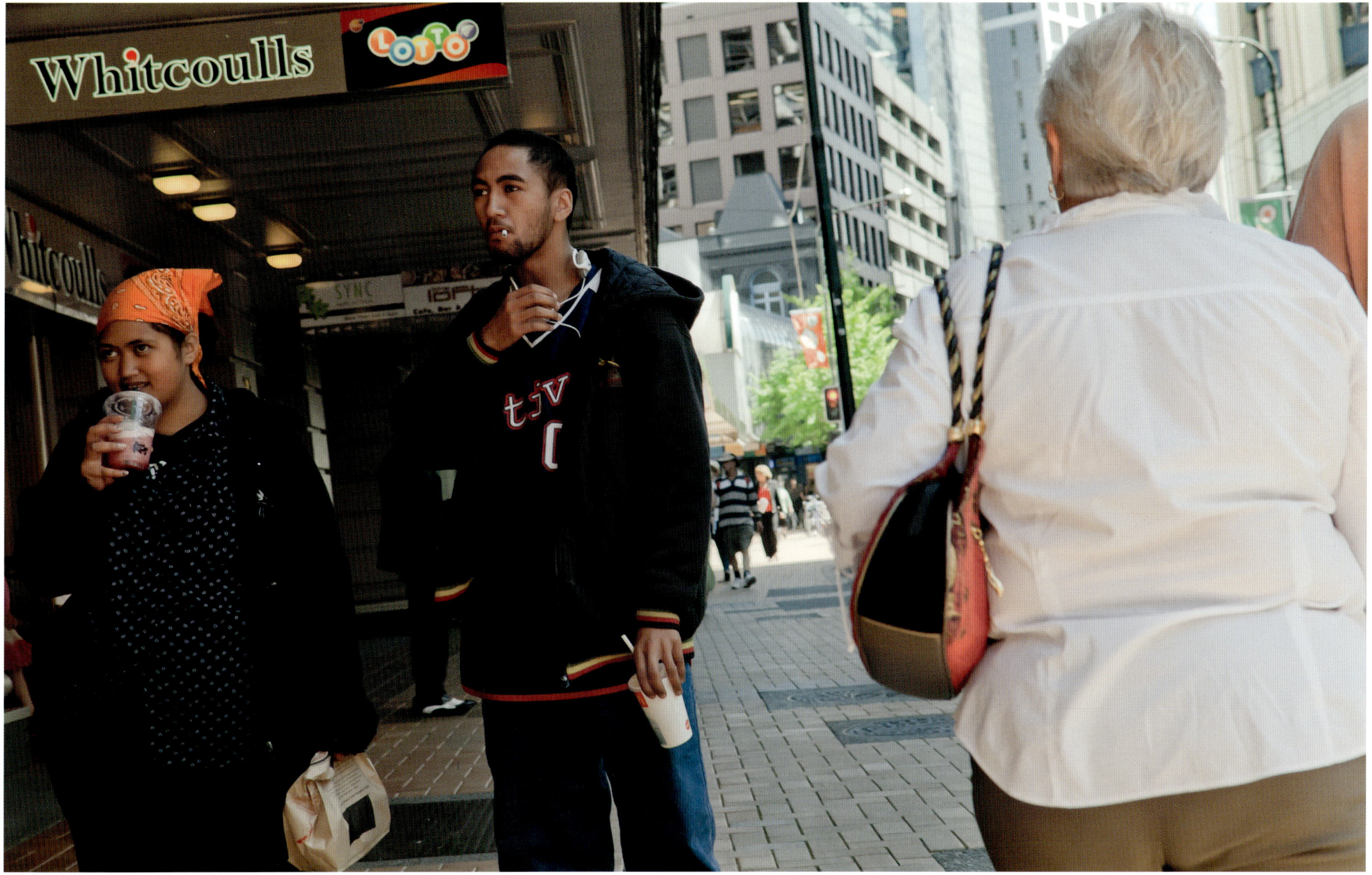
Whitcoulls
LOTTO

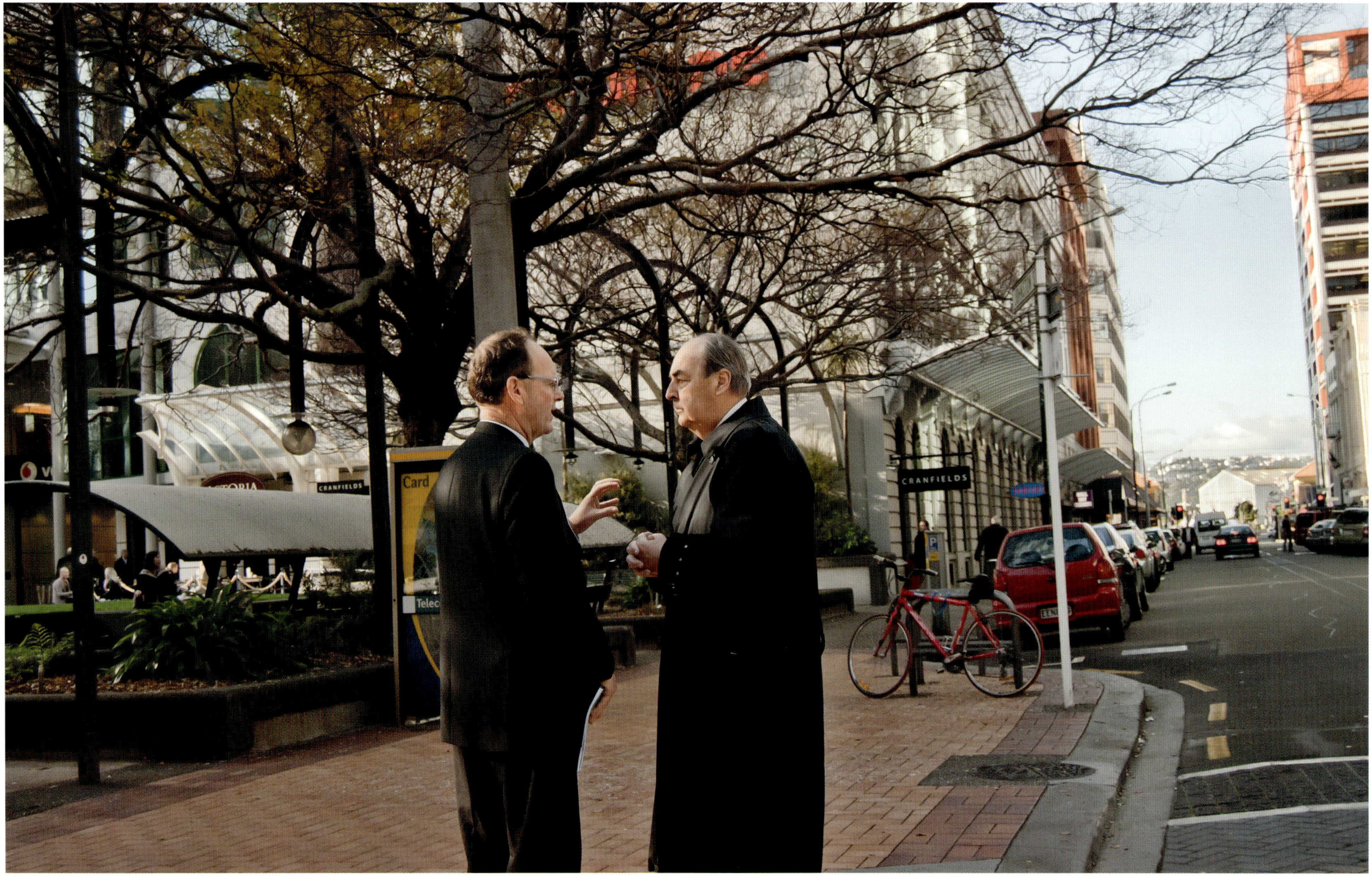
CRANFIELDS
Card
CRANFIELDS

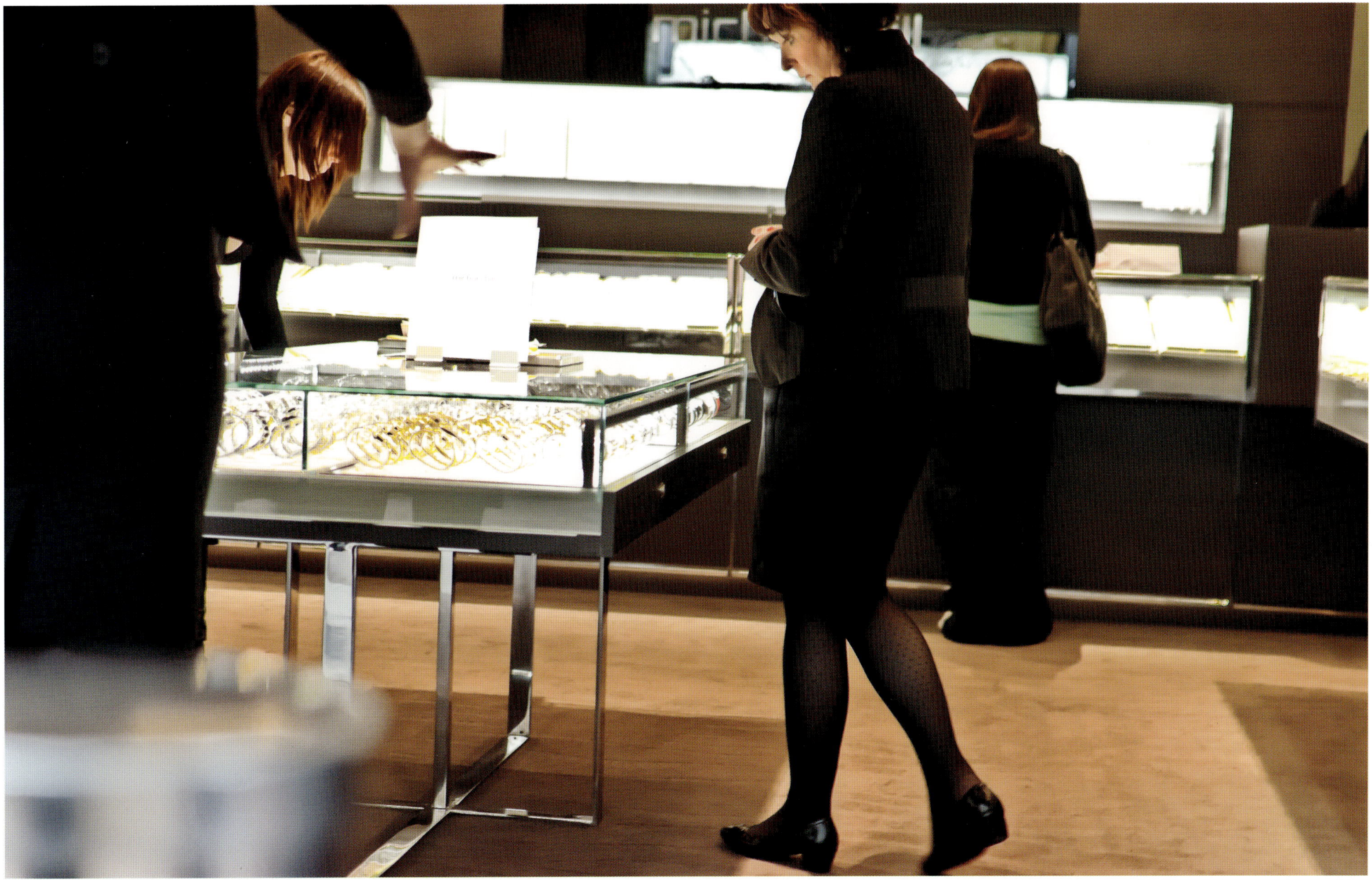

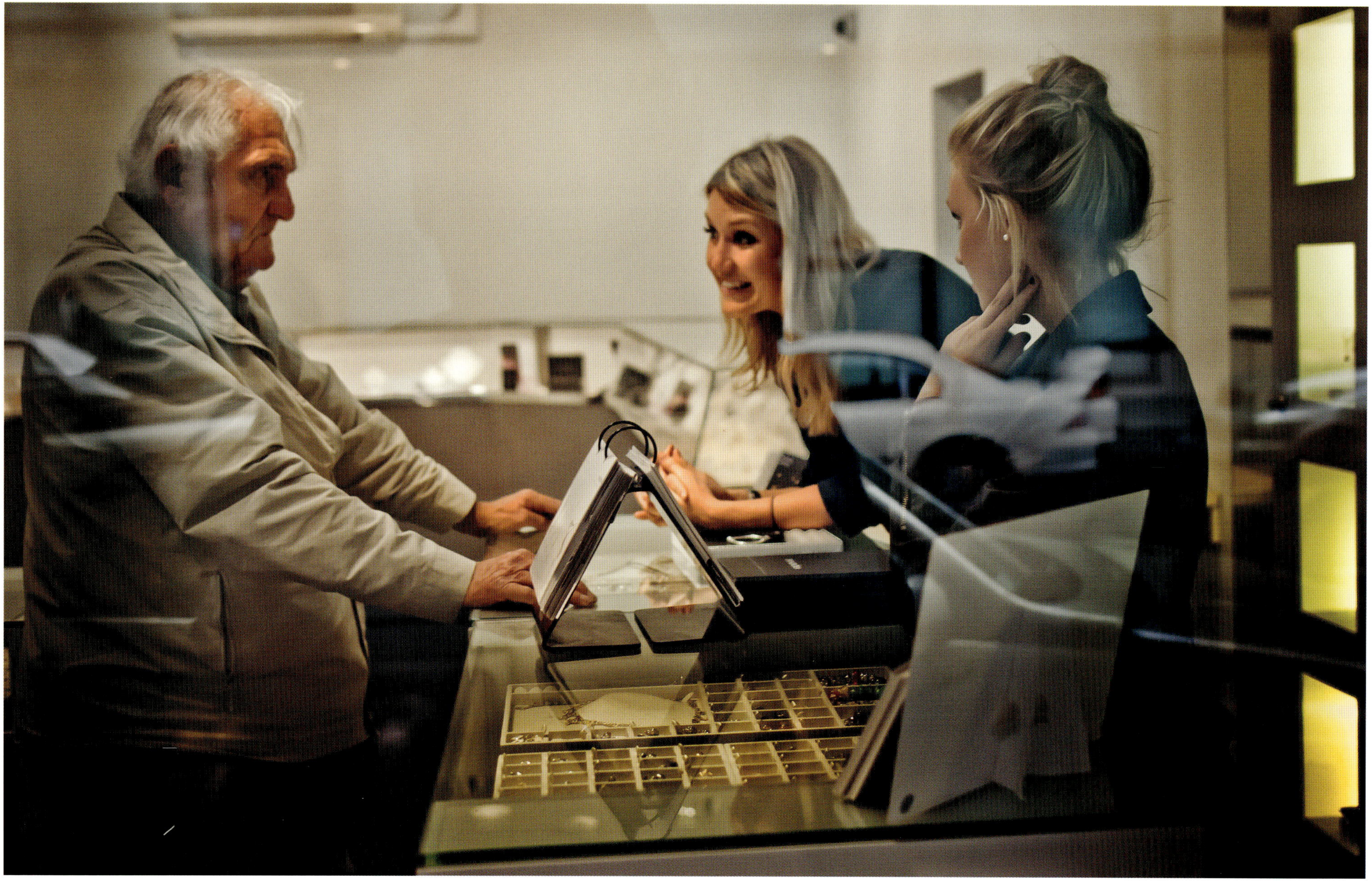

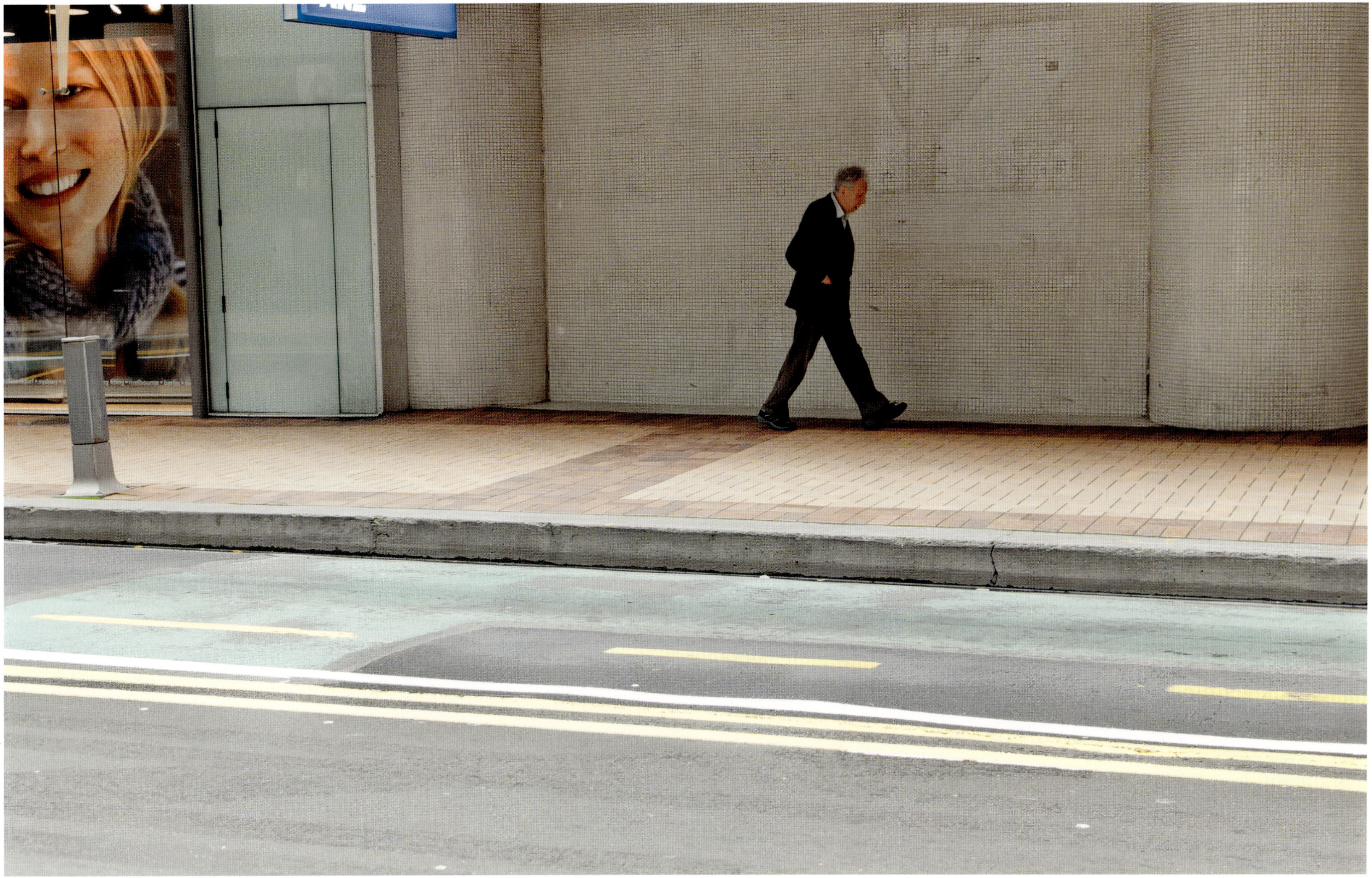

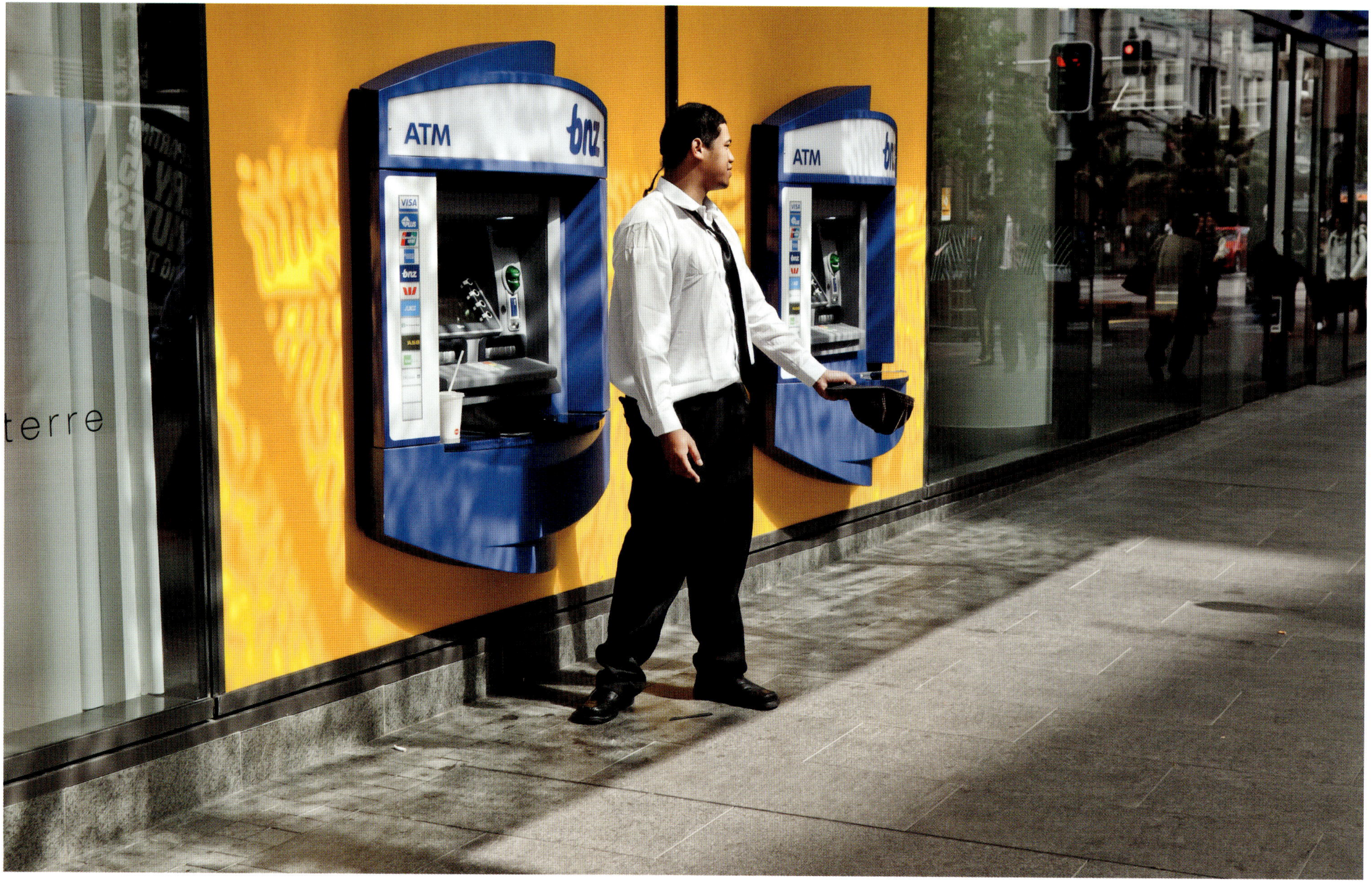
ATM
bnz
ATM
terre

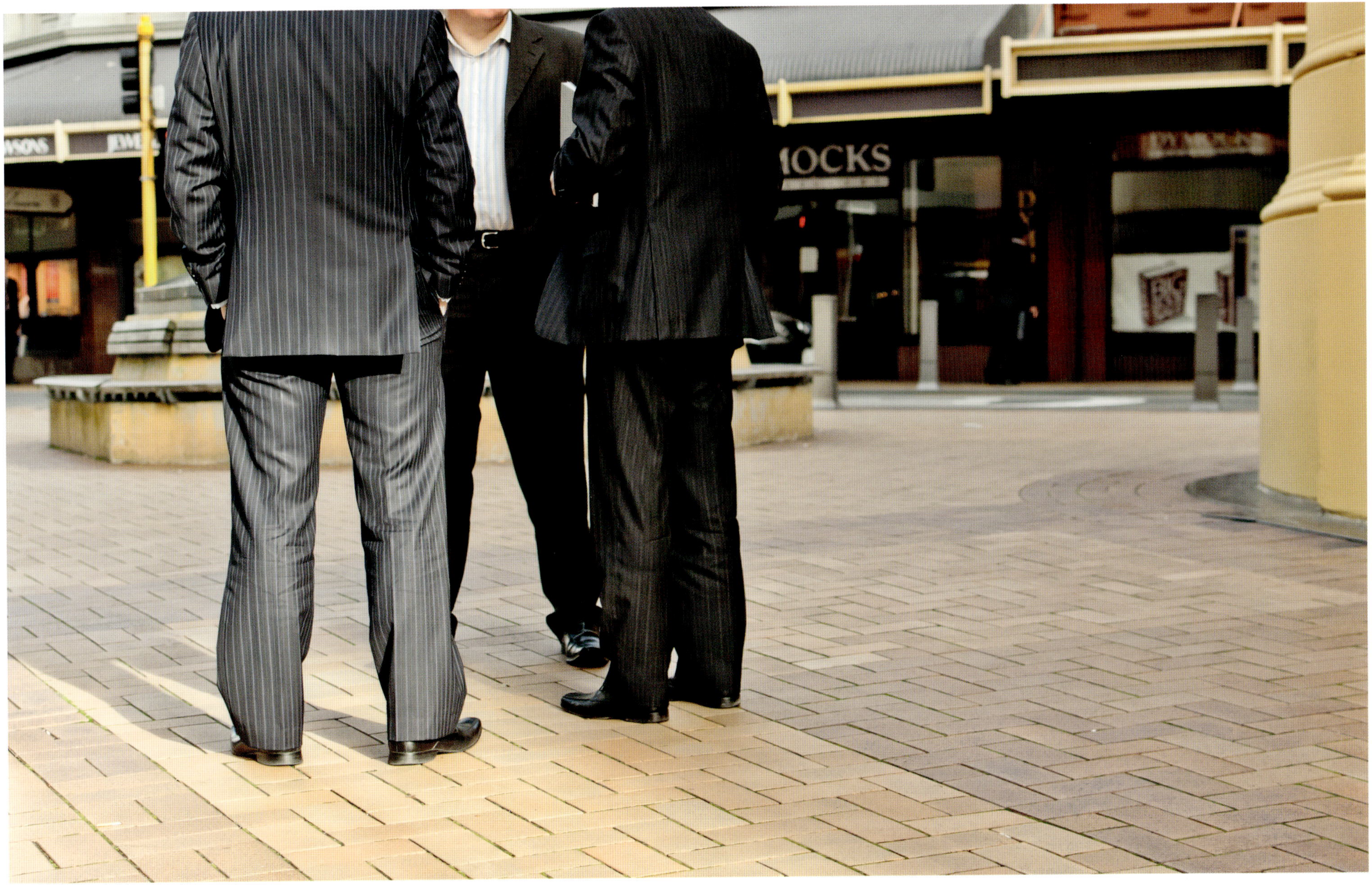
MOCKS

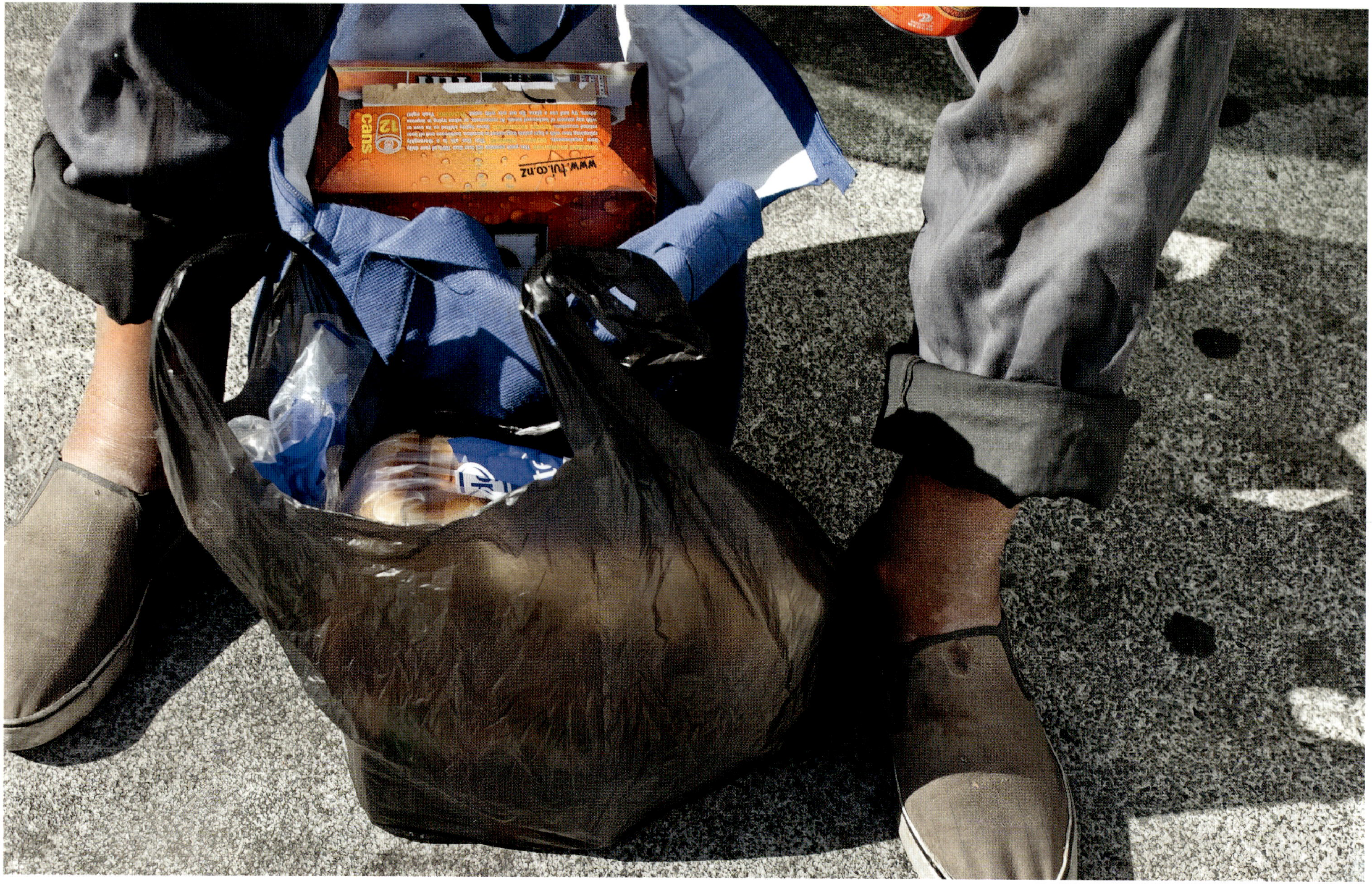

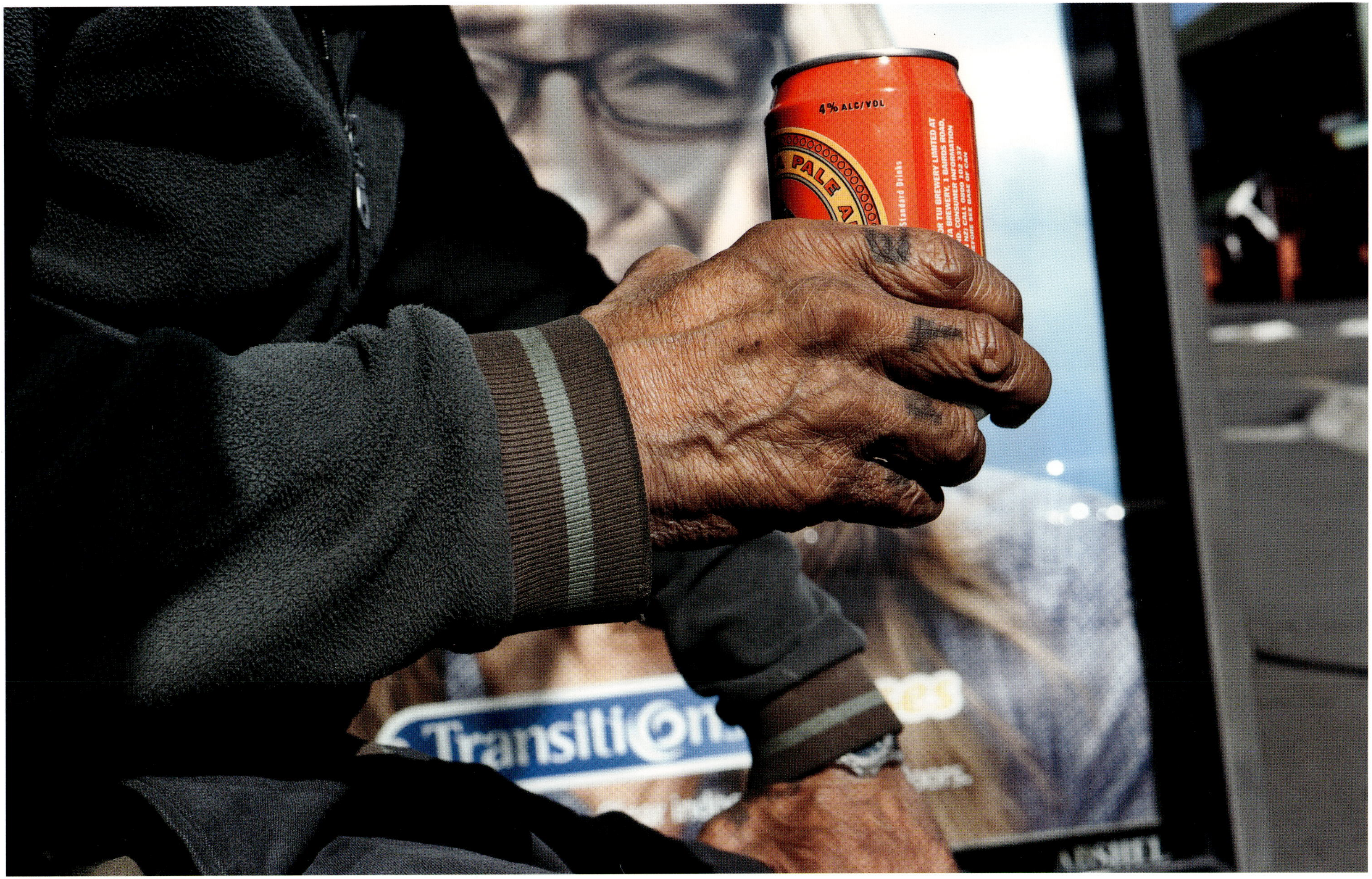
4% ALC/VOL

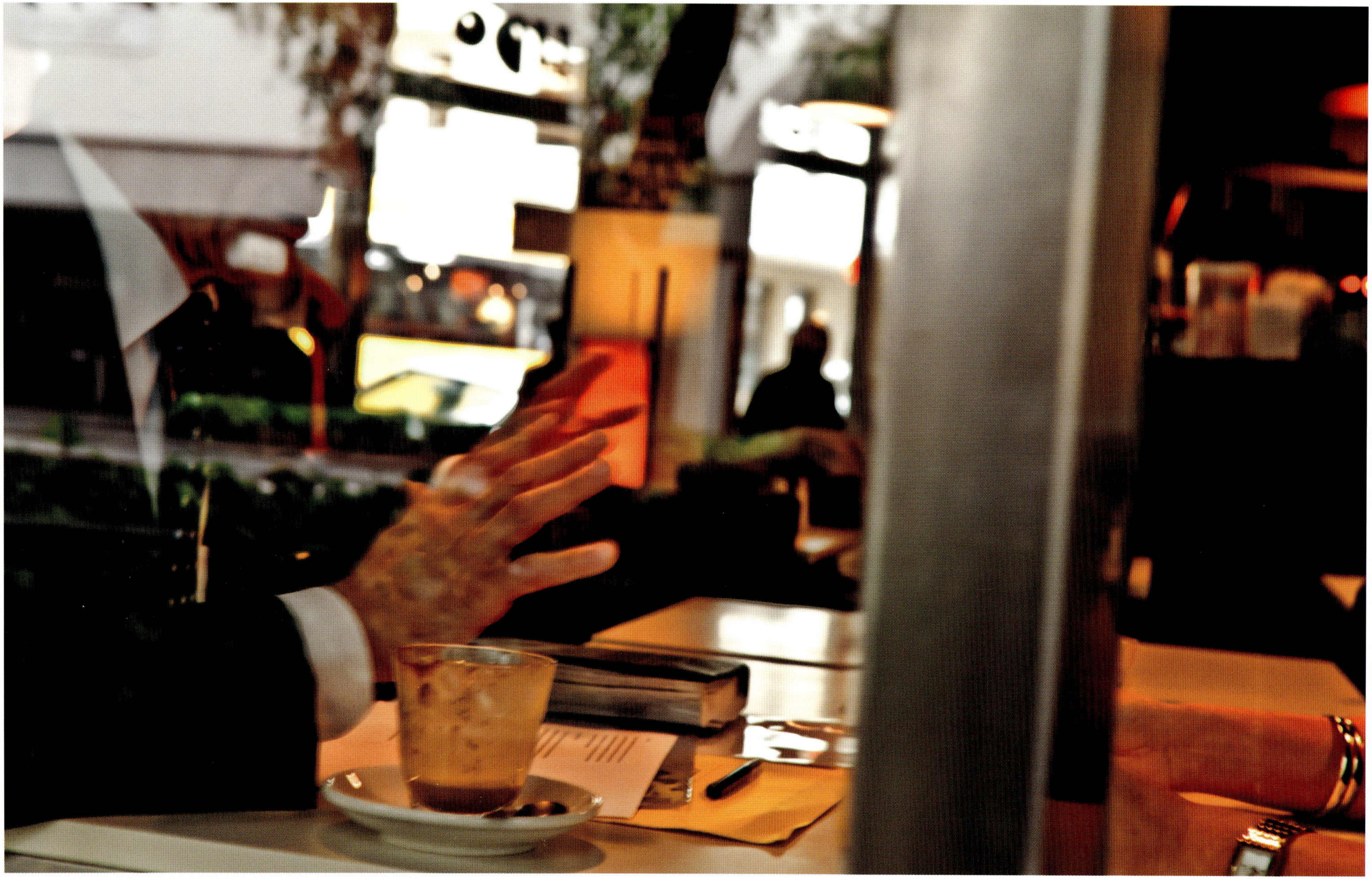

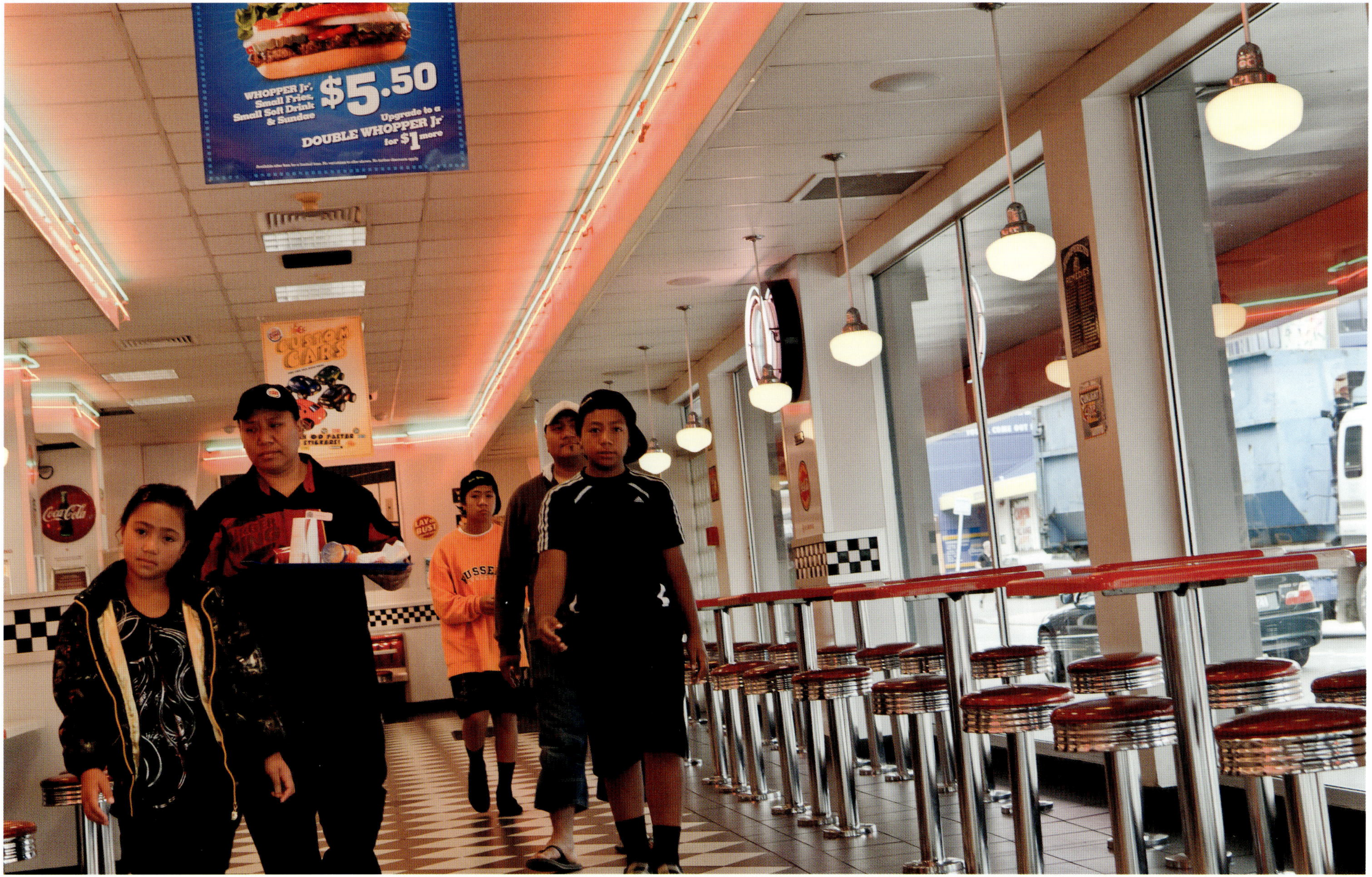
WHOPPER Jr, Small Fries, Small Soft Drink & Sundae
$5.50
Upgrade to a DOUBLE WHOPPER Jr for $1 more
CUSTOM CARS
Coca-Cola

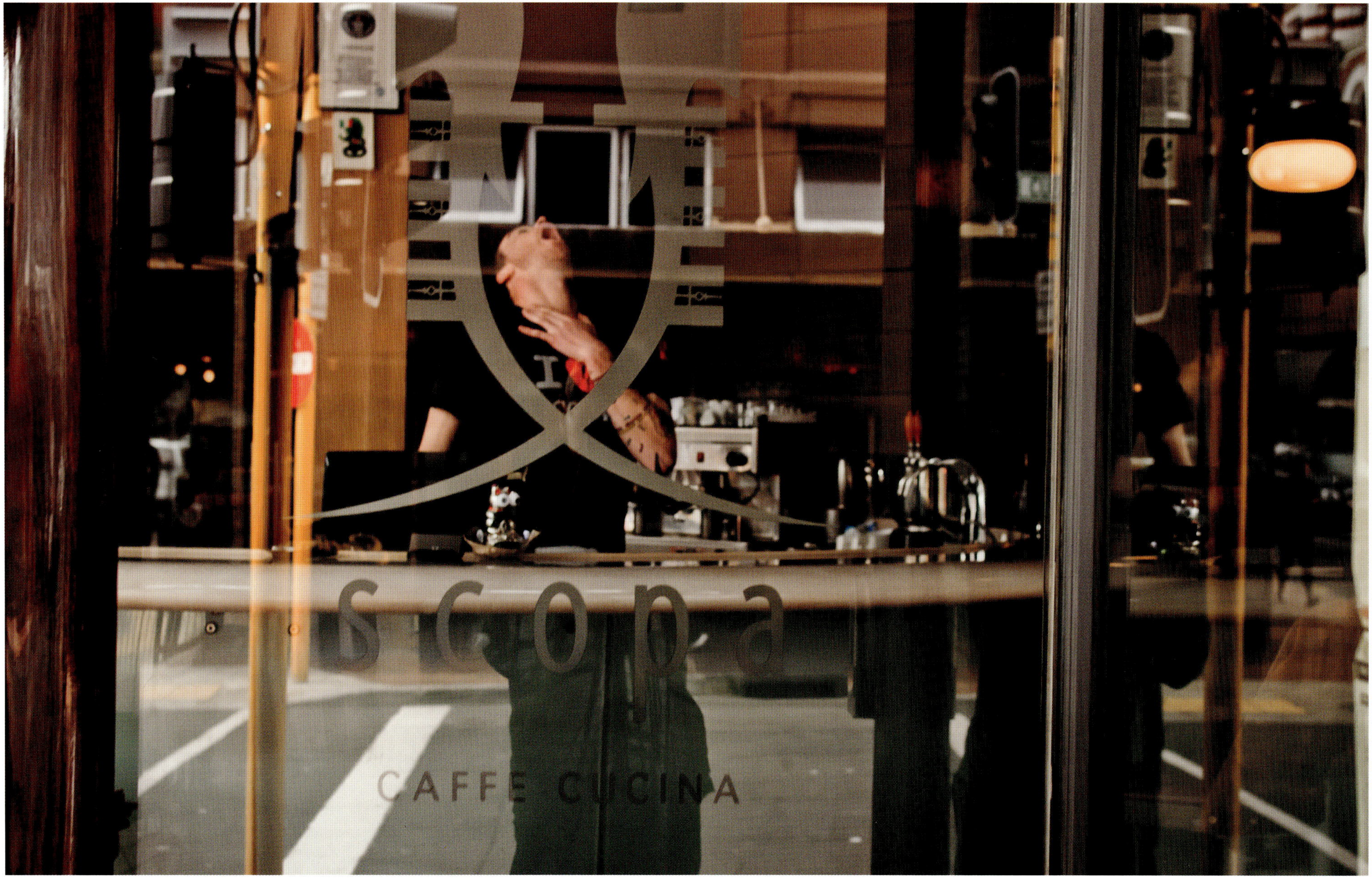
scopa
CAFFE CUCINA

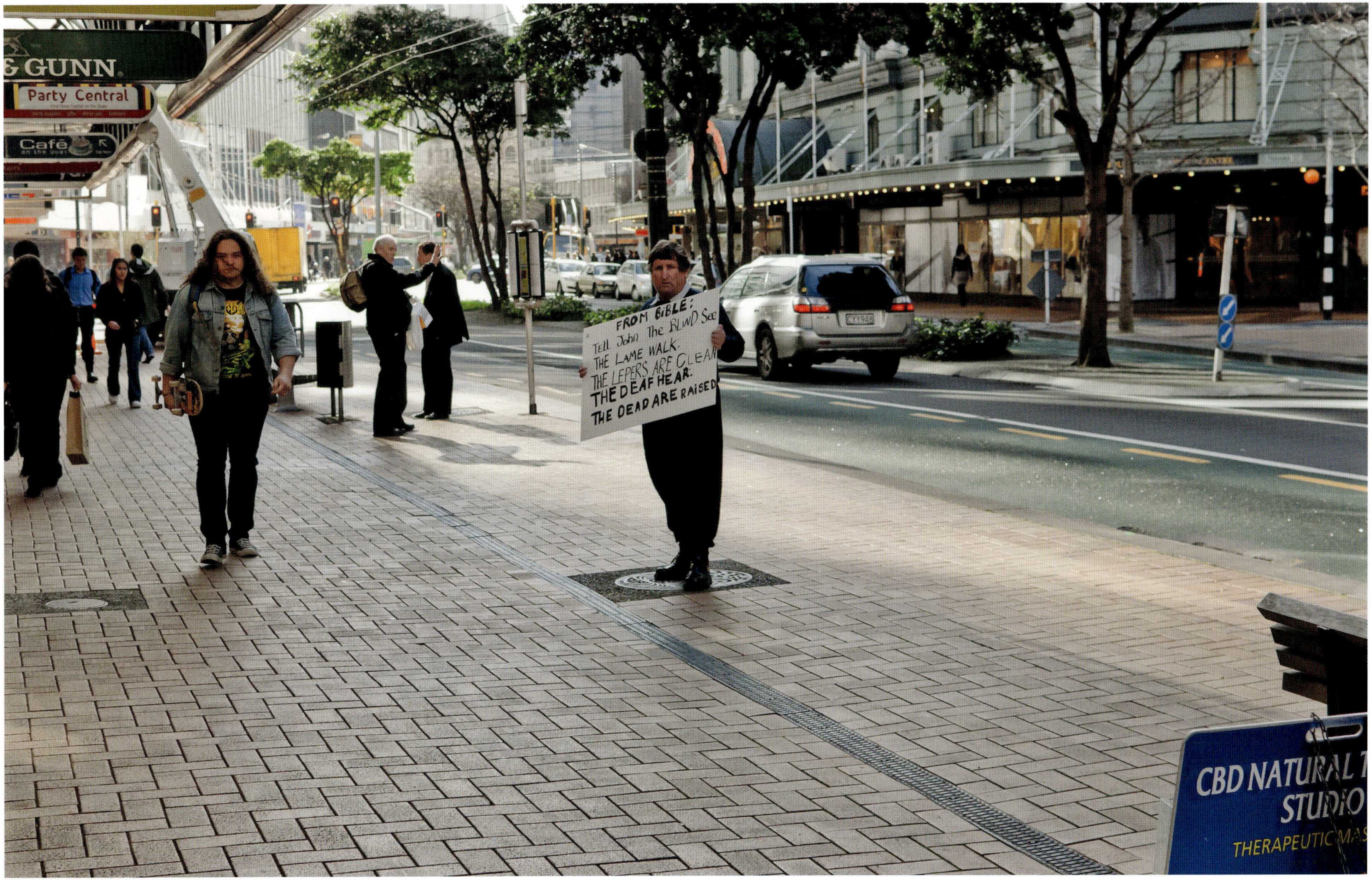
& GUNN
Party Central
Café
FROM BIBLE;
Tell John The BLIND See
THE LAME WALK.
THE LEPERS ARE CLEAN
THE DEAF HEAR.
THE DEAD ARE RAISED
CBD NATURAL
STUDIO
THERAPEUTIC

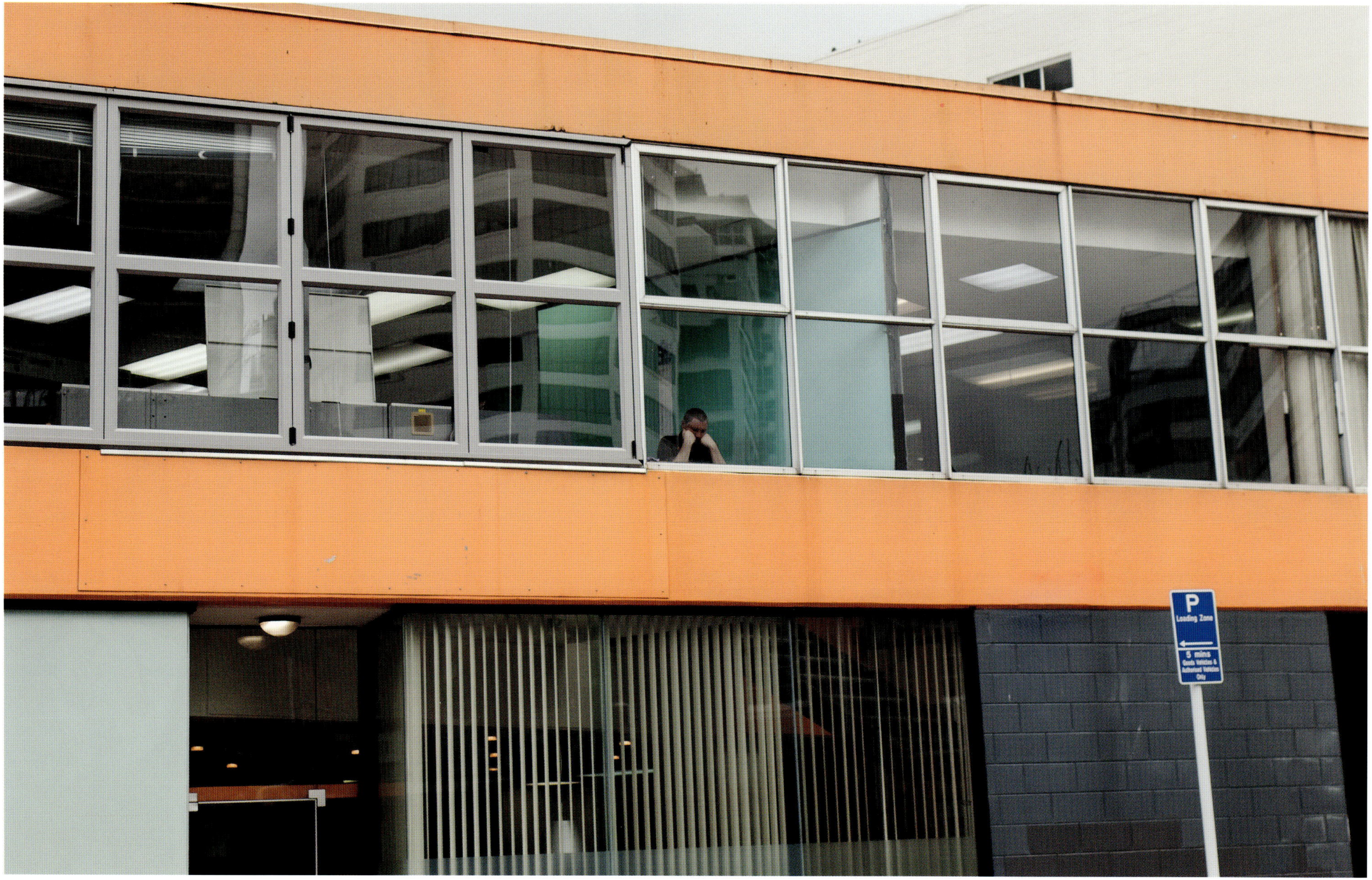
P
Loading Zone
5 mins

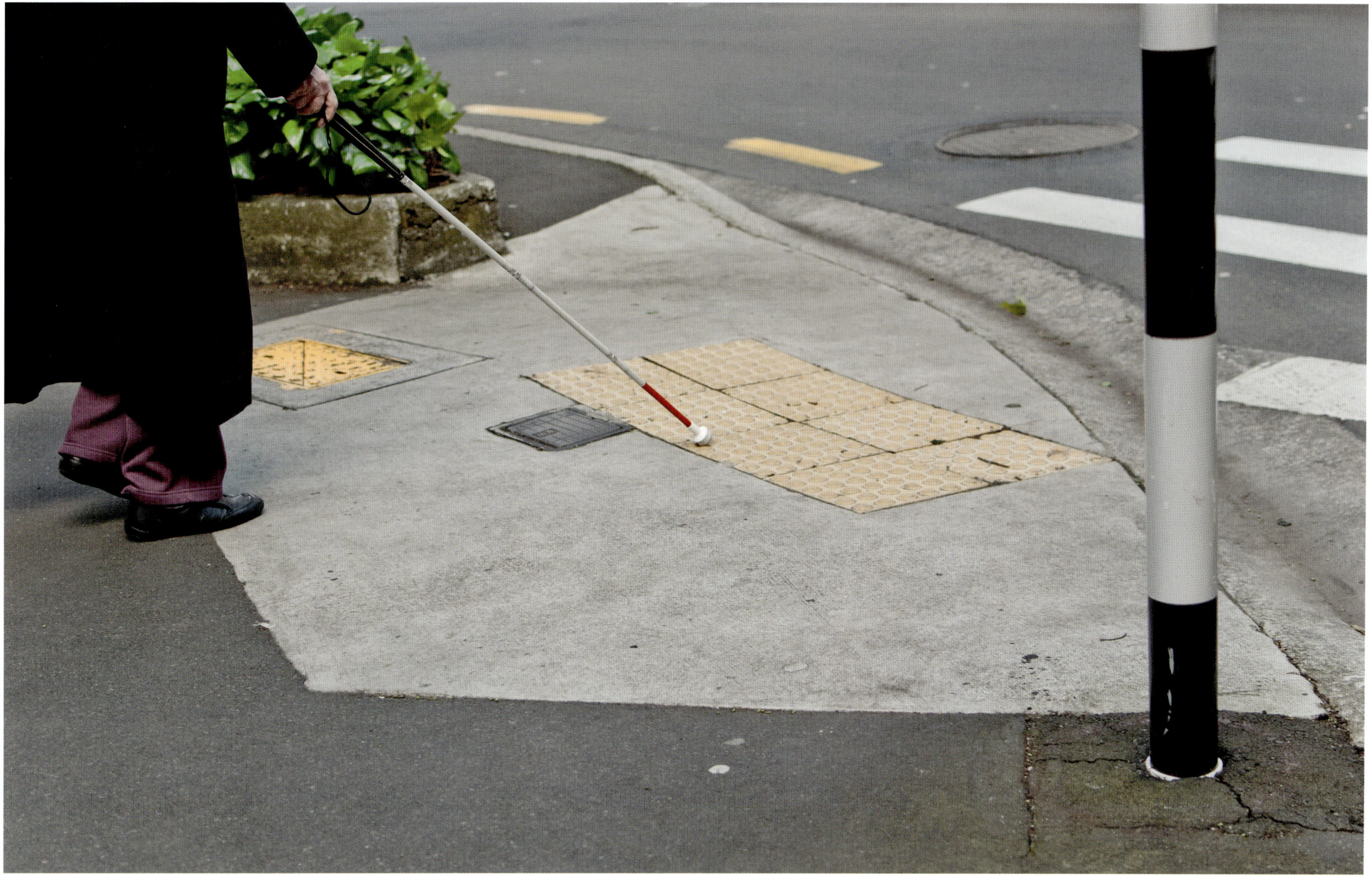

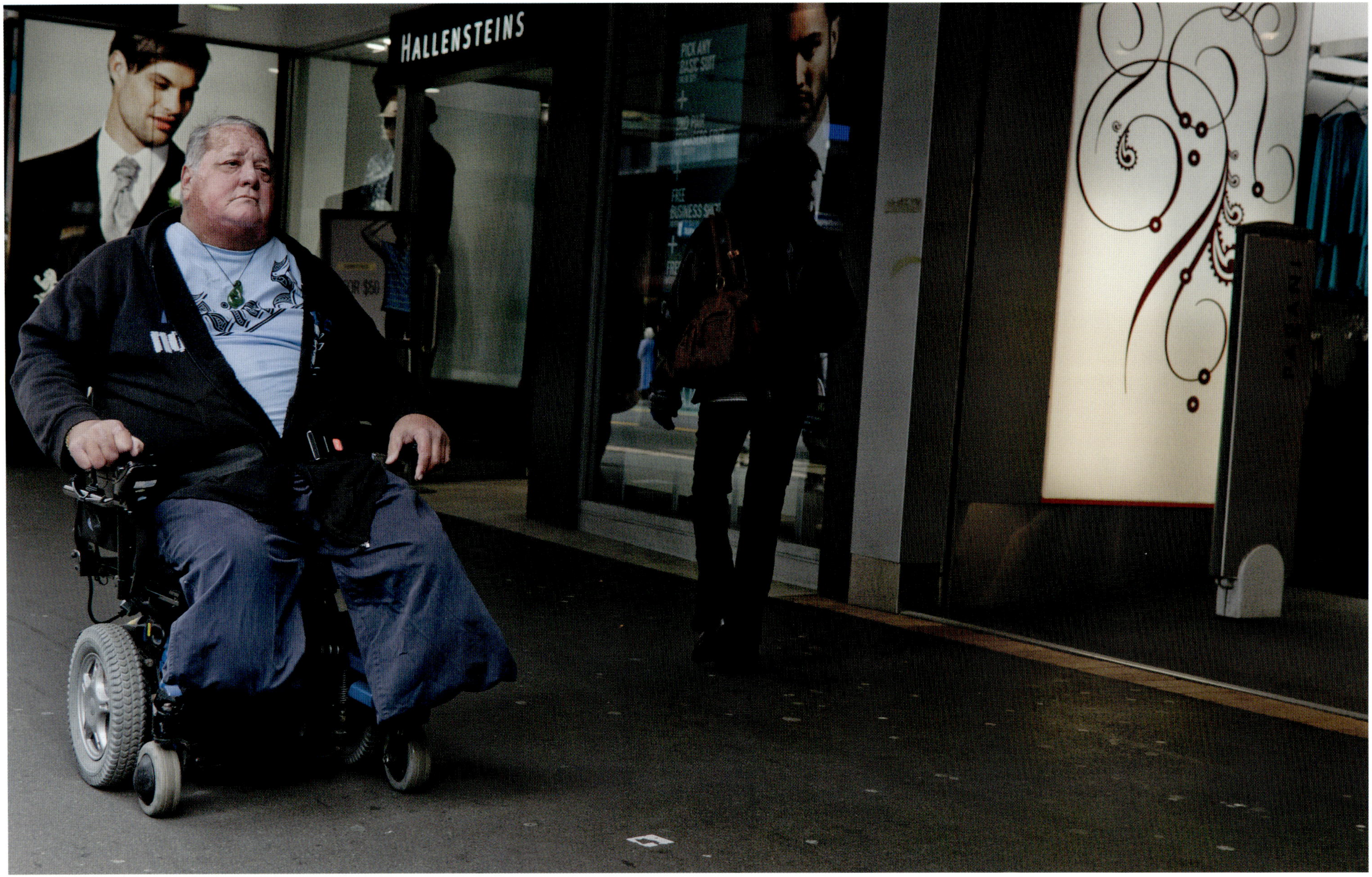
HALLENSTEINS

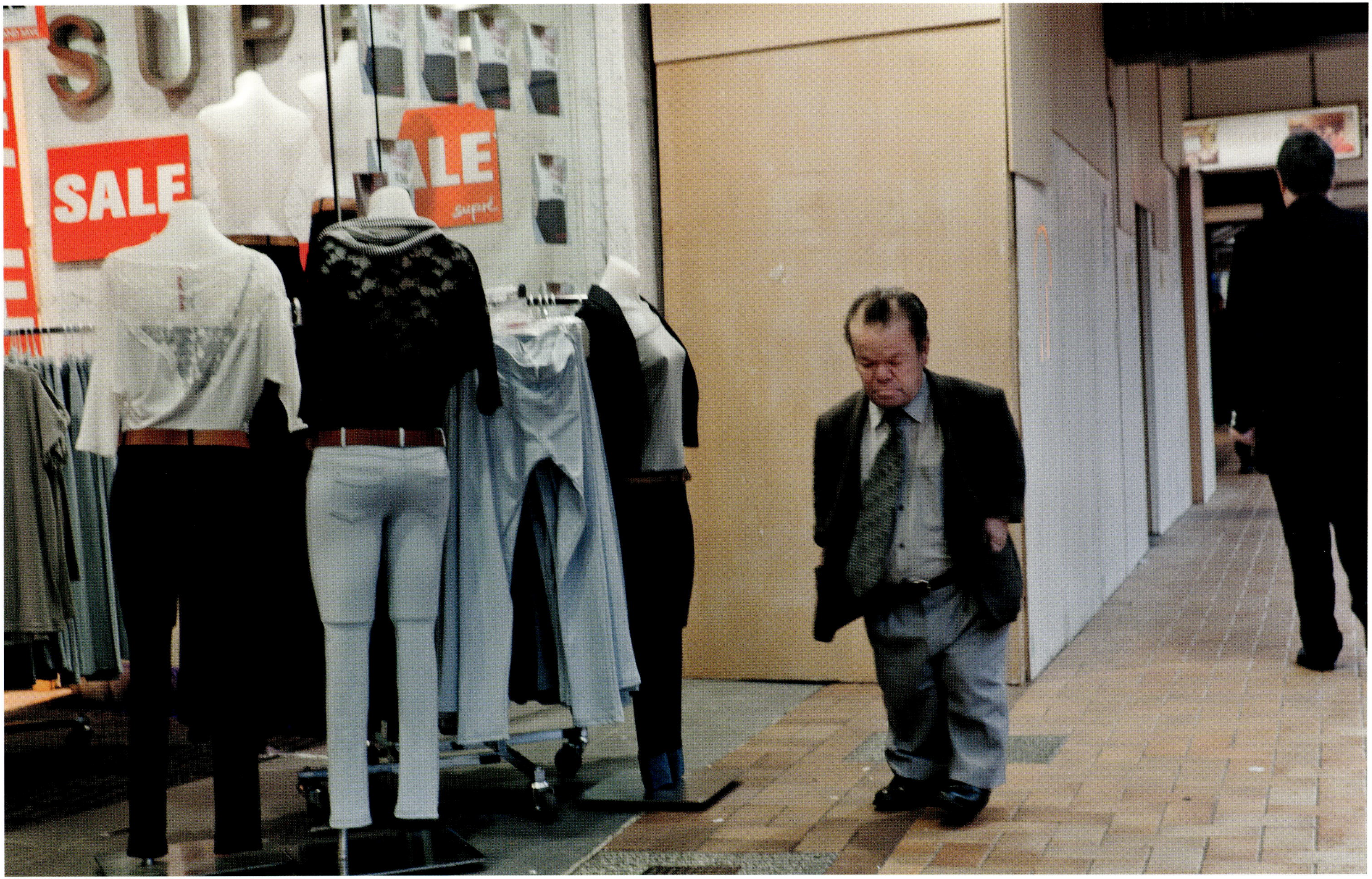
SUP
SALE
ALE

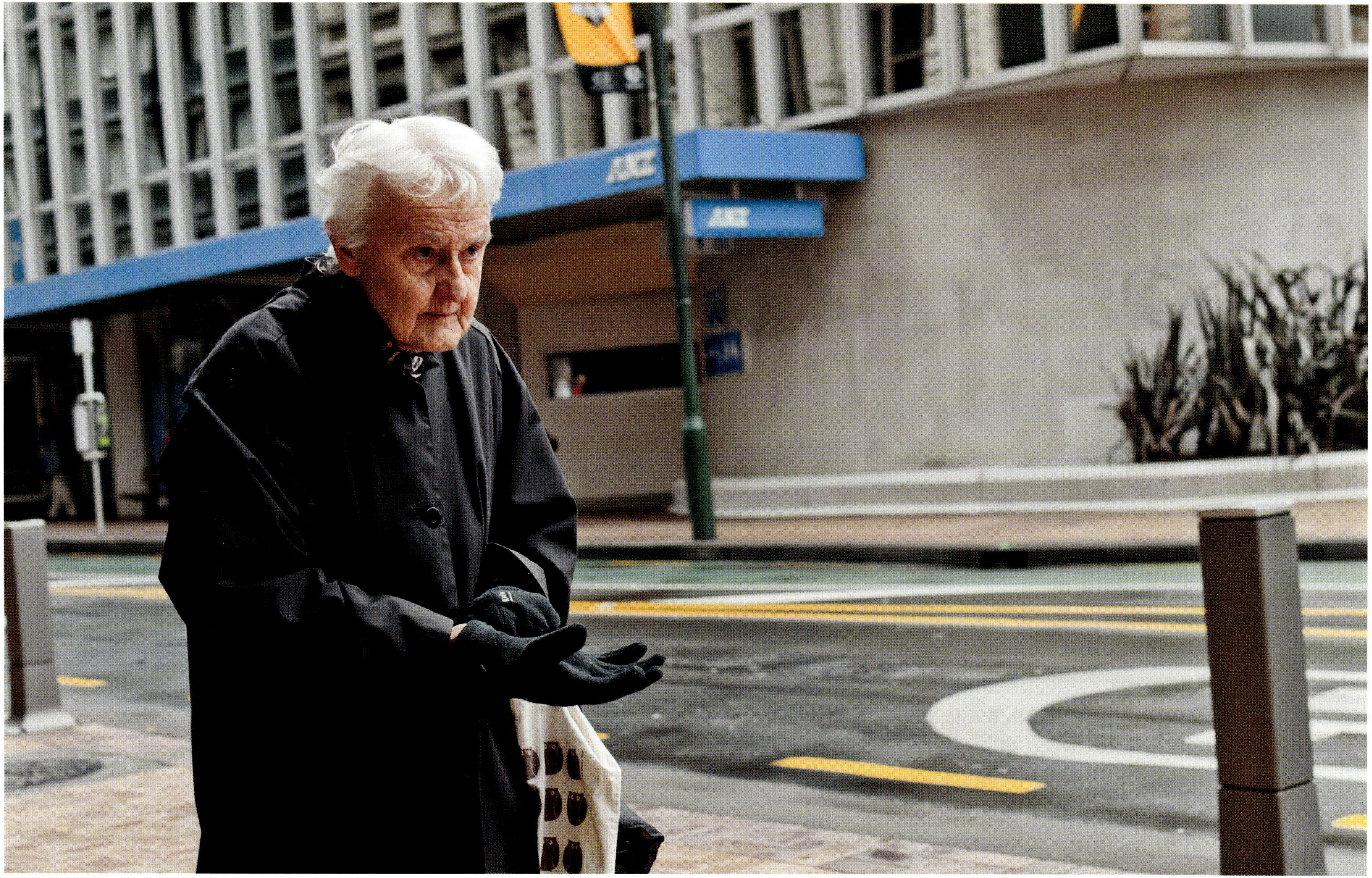
ANZ
ANZ

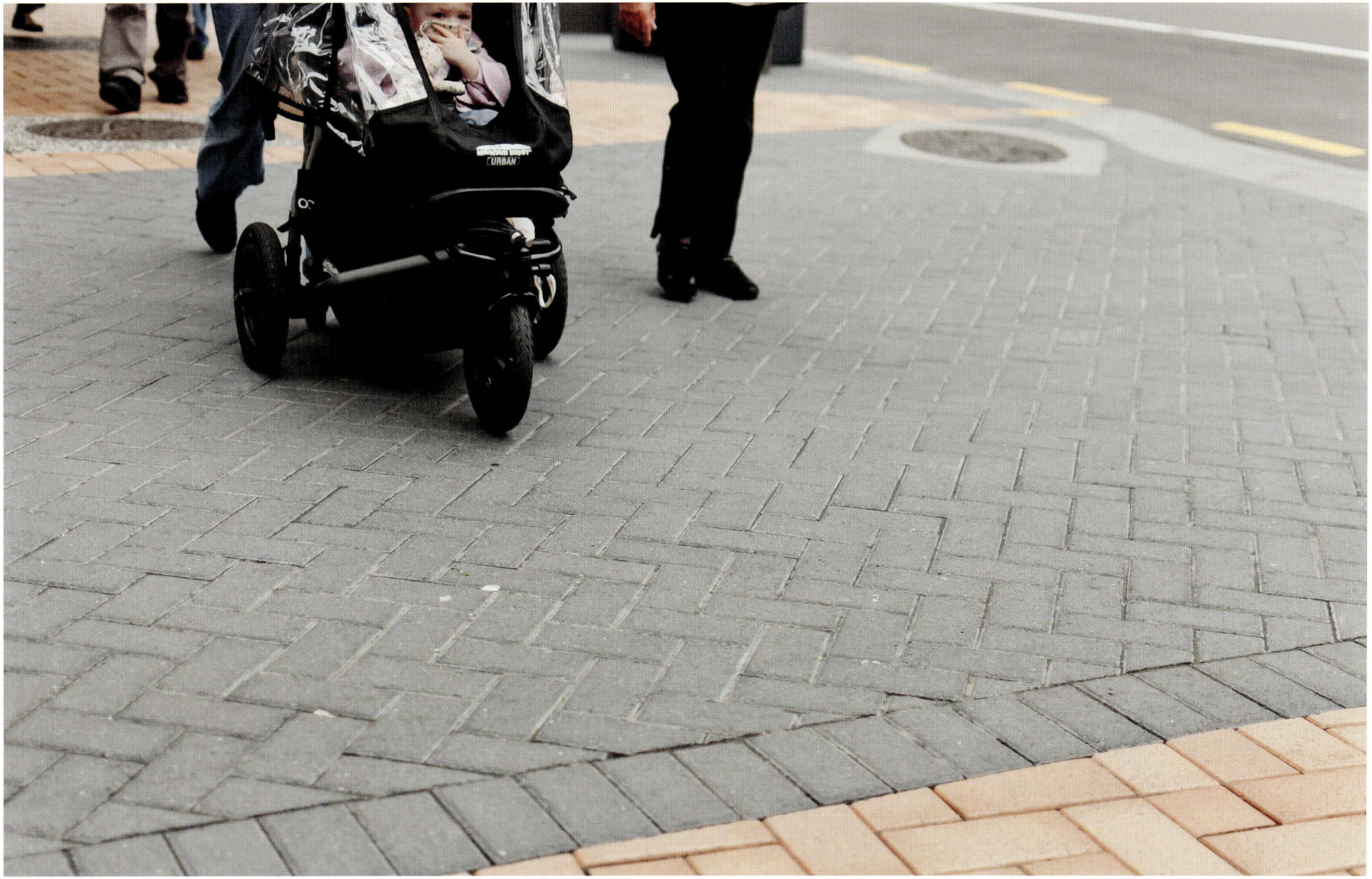
URBAN

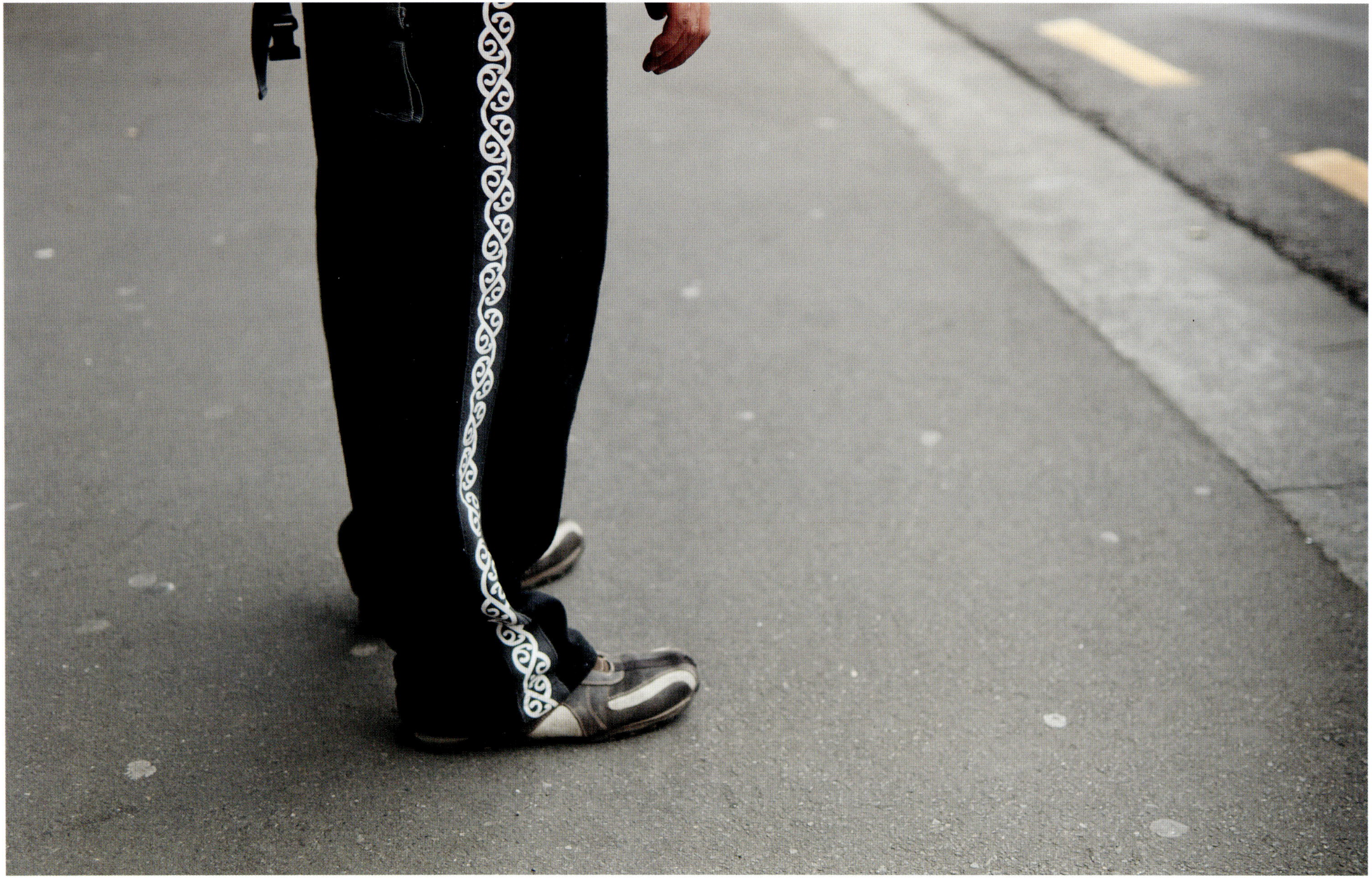

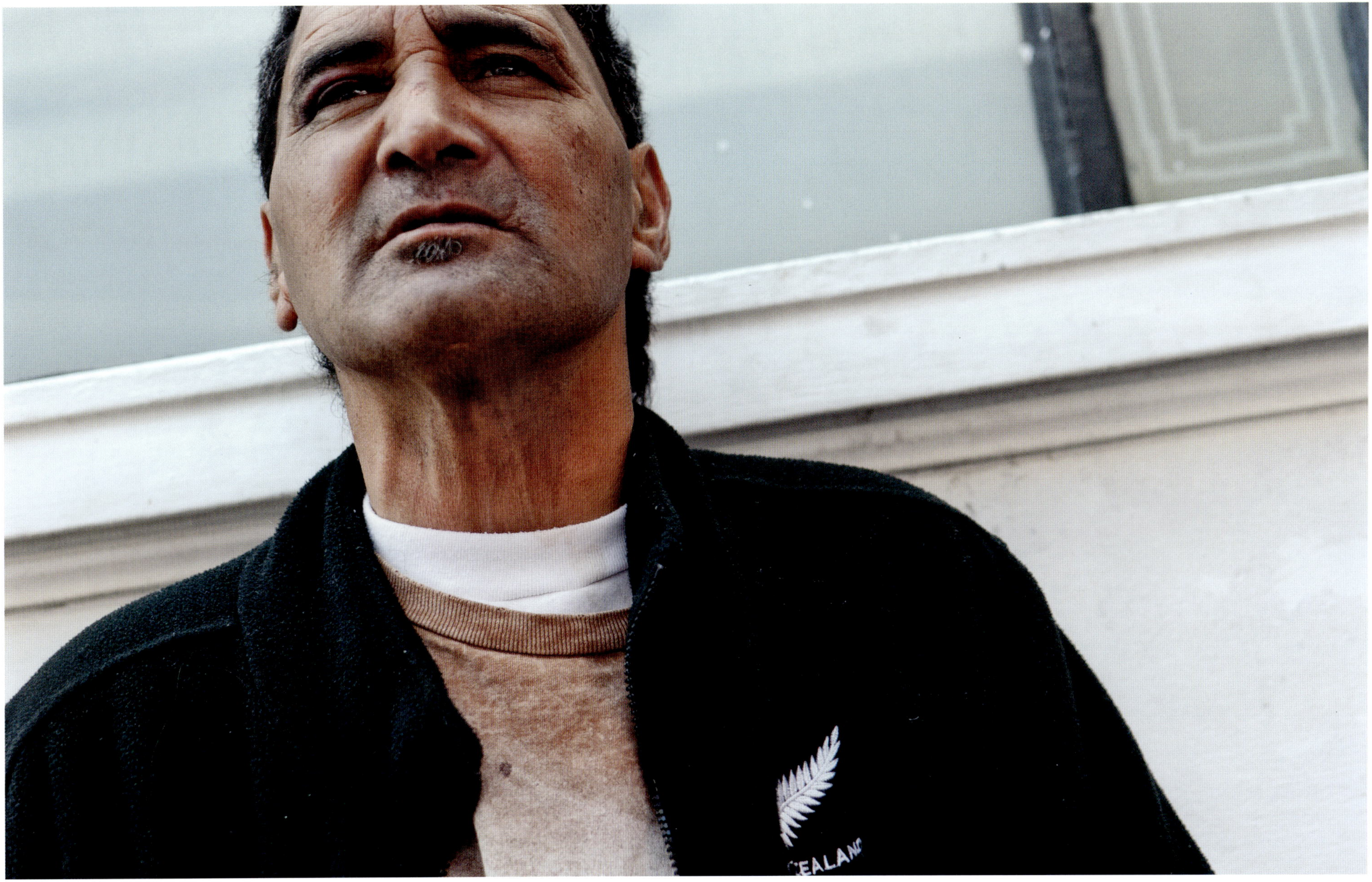

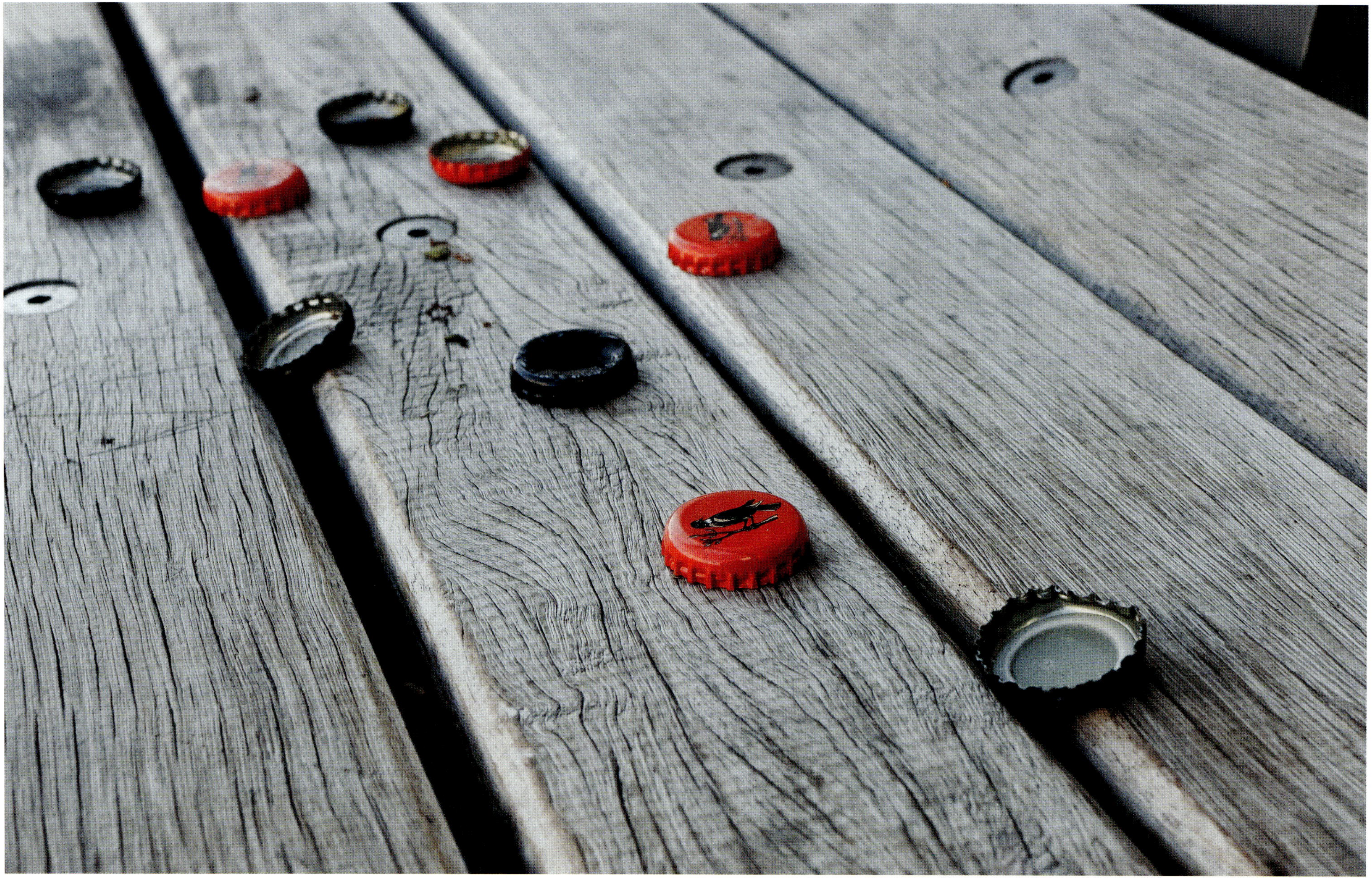

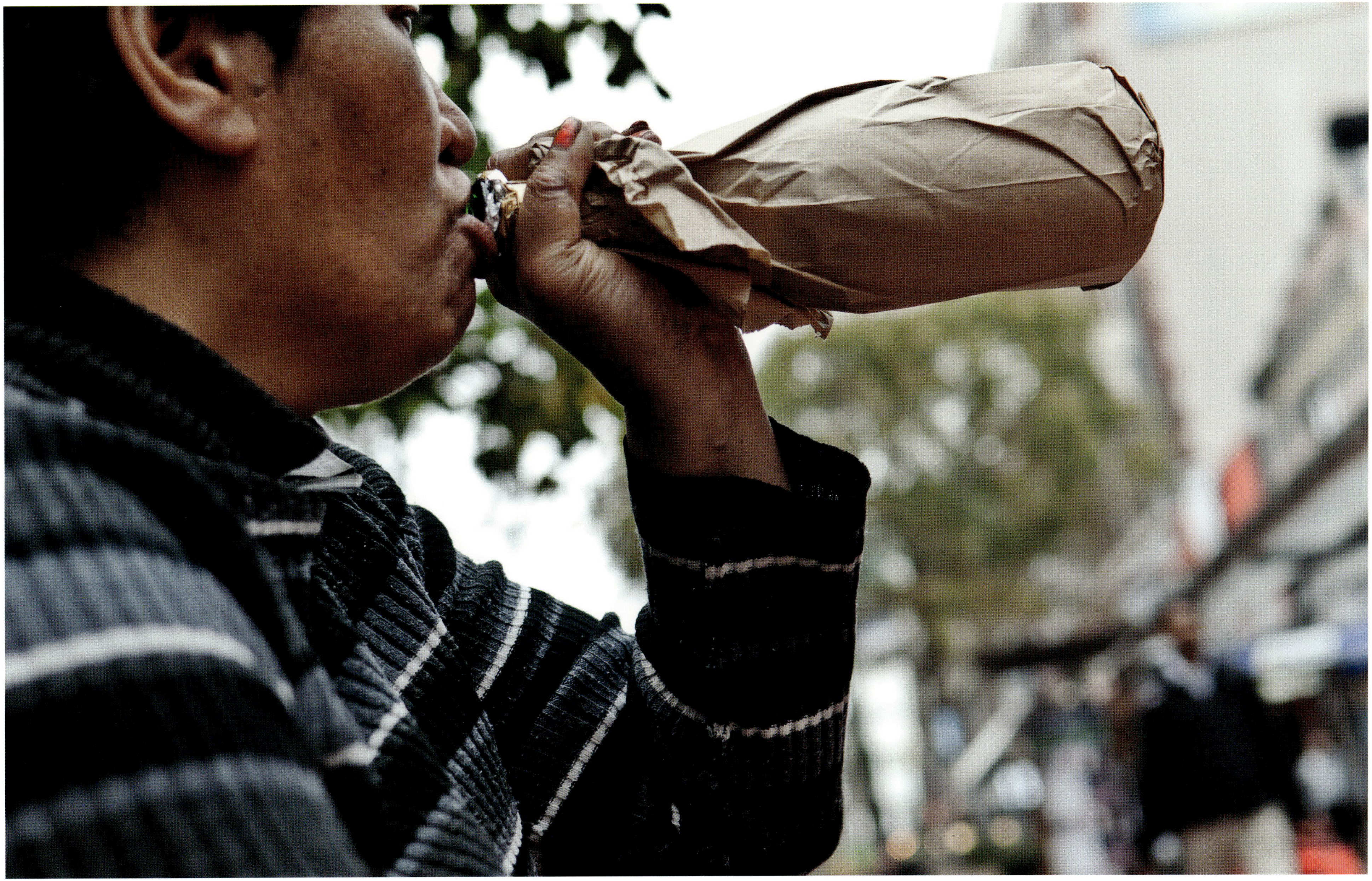

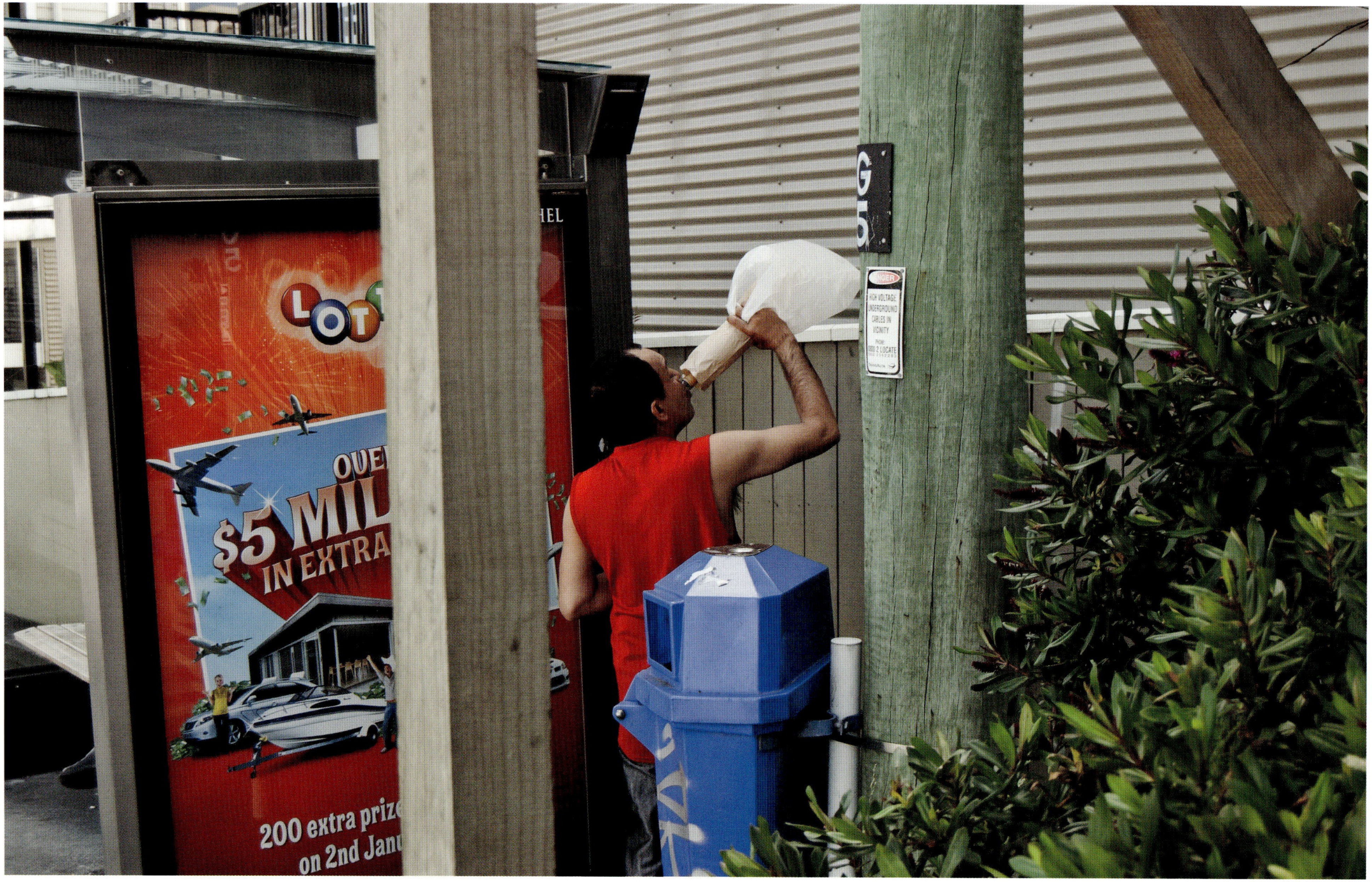

HEL
LOTT
$5 MIL
IN EXTRA
200 extra prize
on 2nd Janu
G
5
HIGH VOLTAGE
UNDERGROUND
CABLES IN
VICINITY

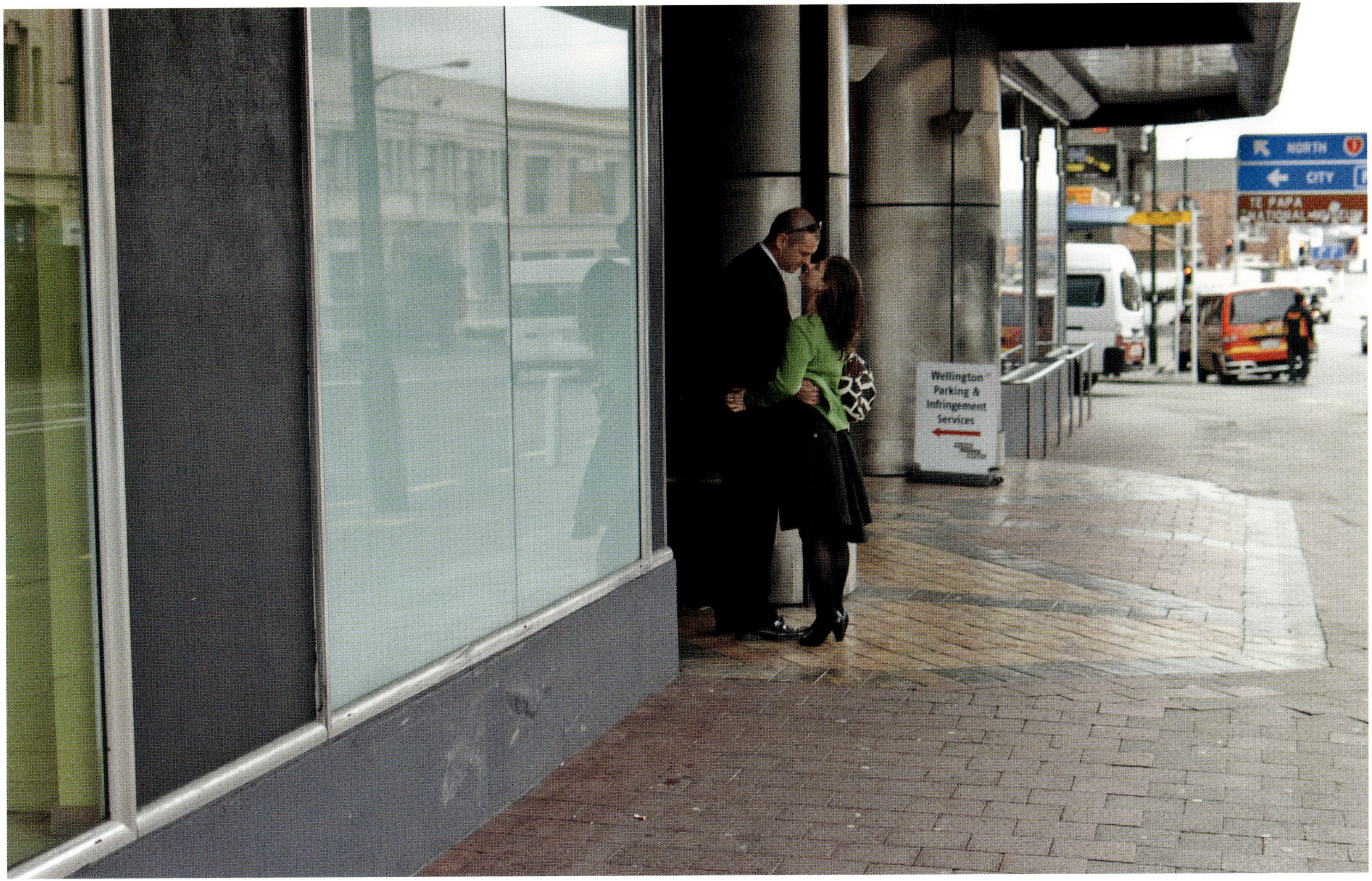
NORTH
CITY
Wellington
Parking &
Infringement
Services

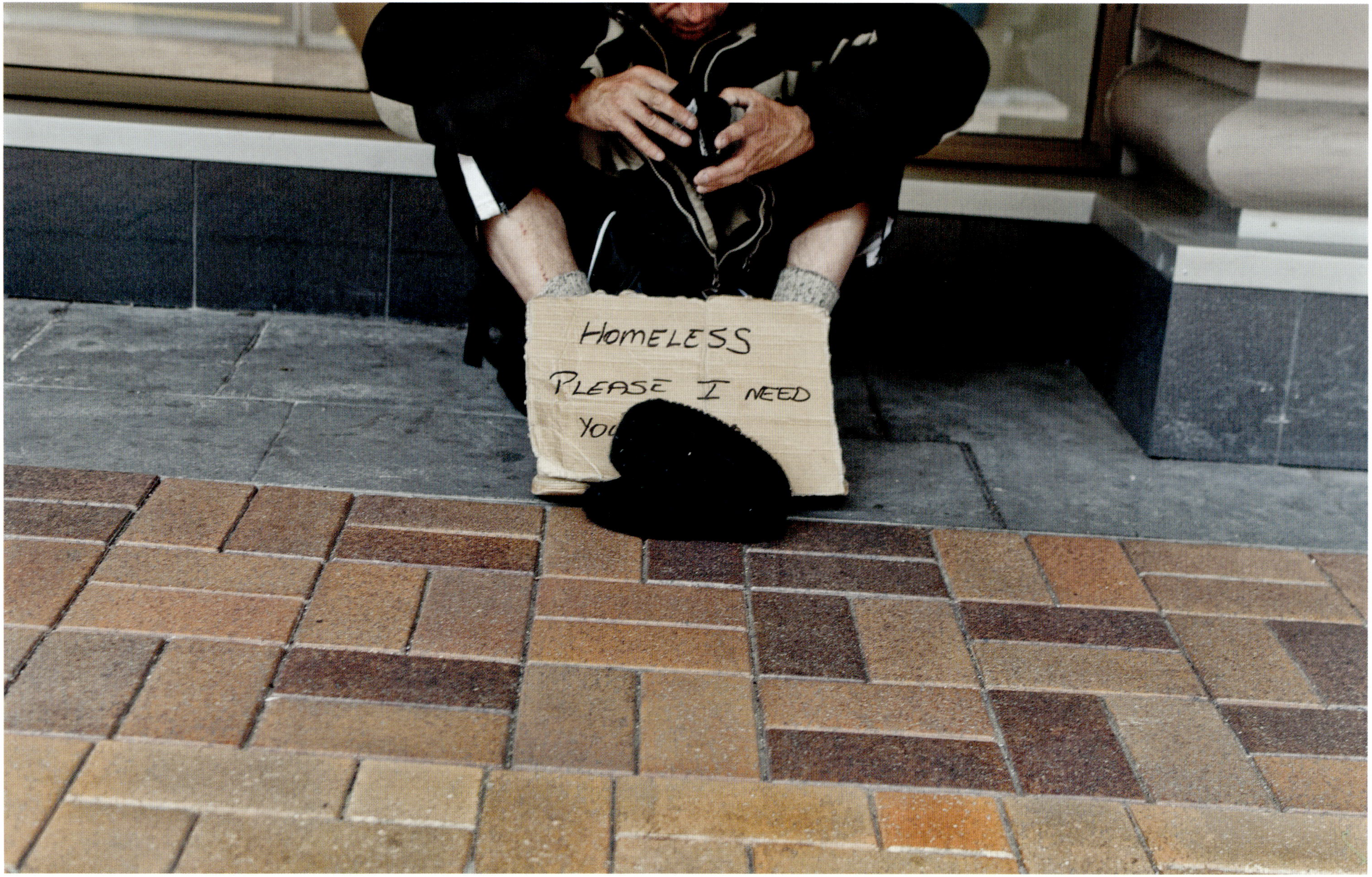
HOMELESS
PLEASE I NEED

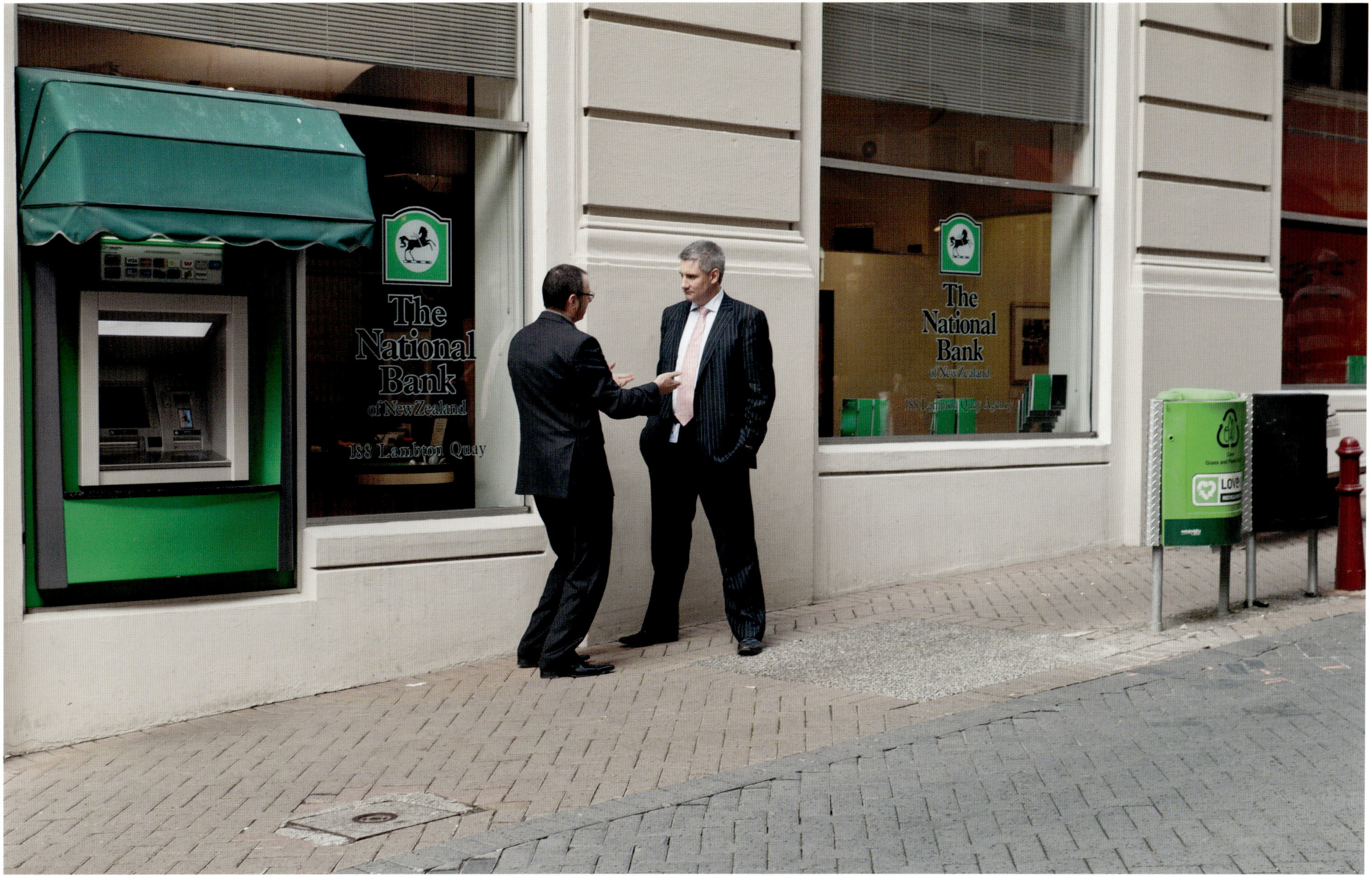
The National Bank
of NewZealand
188 Lambton Quay
The National Bank
of NewZealand

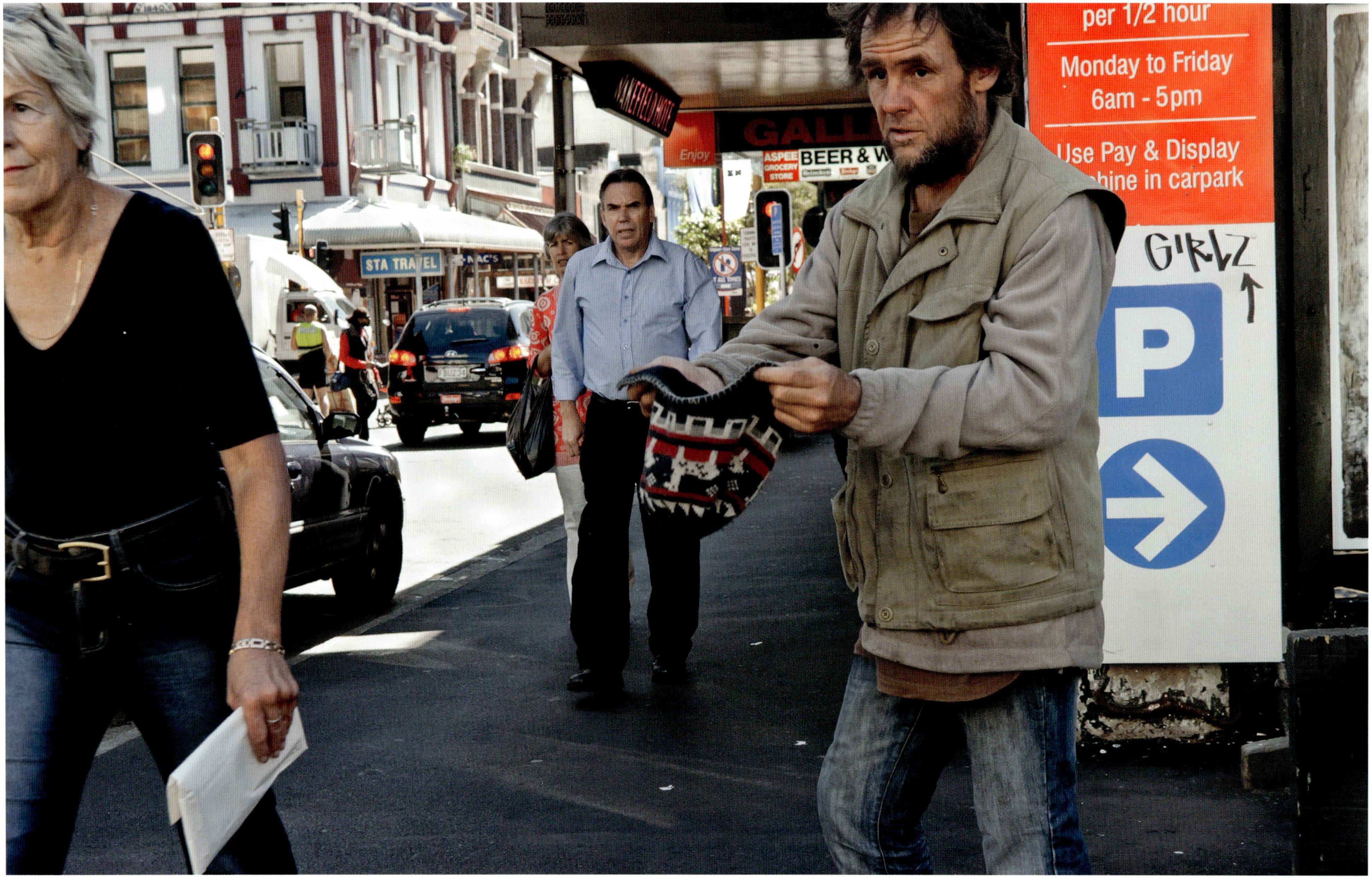
per 1/2 hour
Monday to Friday
6am - 5pm
Use Pay & Display
in carpark
GIRLZ
P
STA TRAVEL
Enjoy

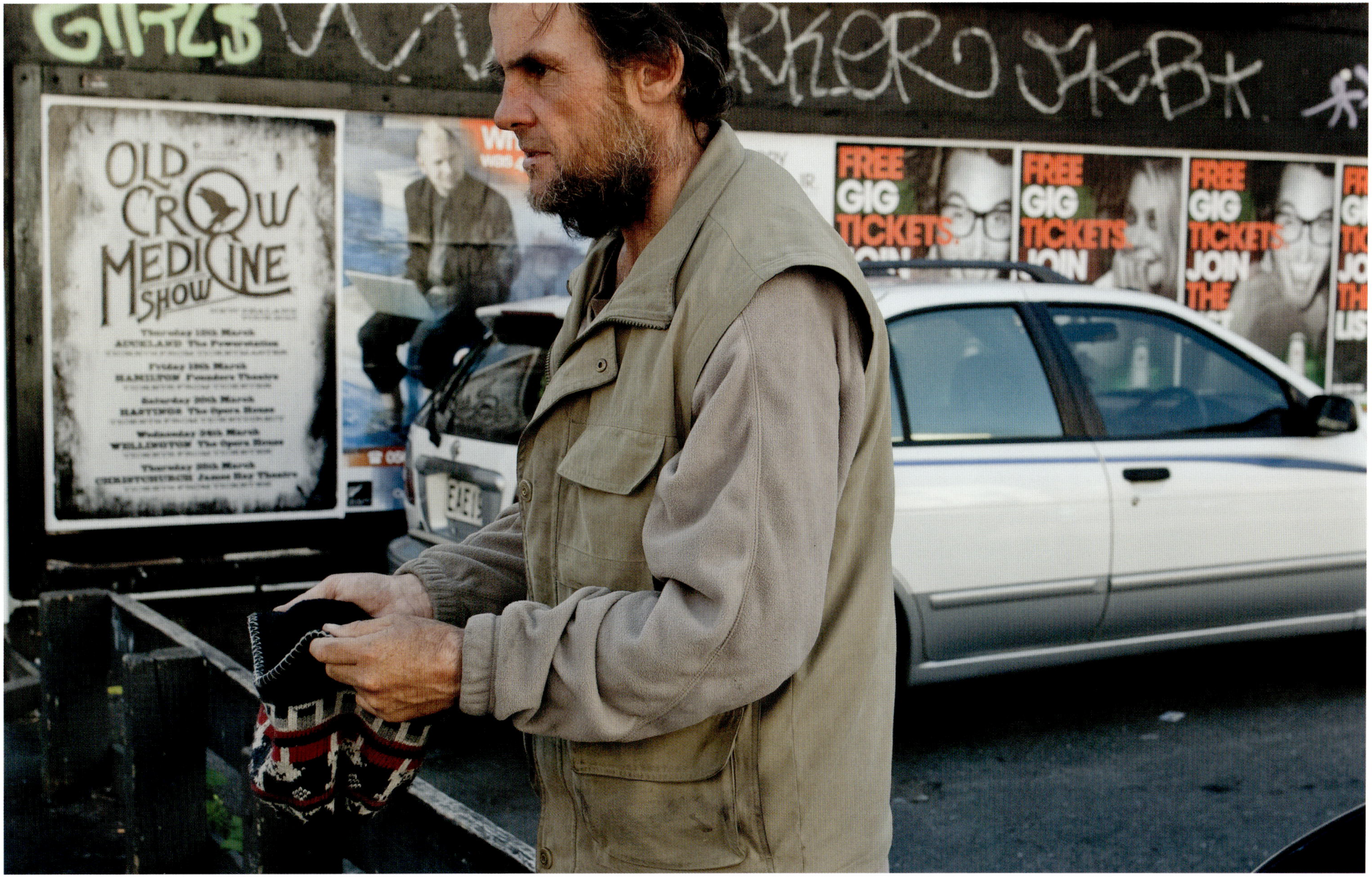
OLD CROW MEDICINE SHOW
FREE GIG TICKETS. JOIN
FREE GIG TICKETS JOIN
FREE GIG TICKETS. JOIN THE

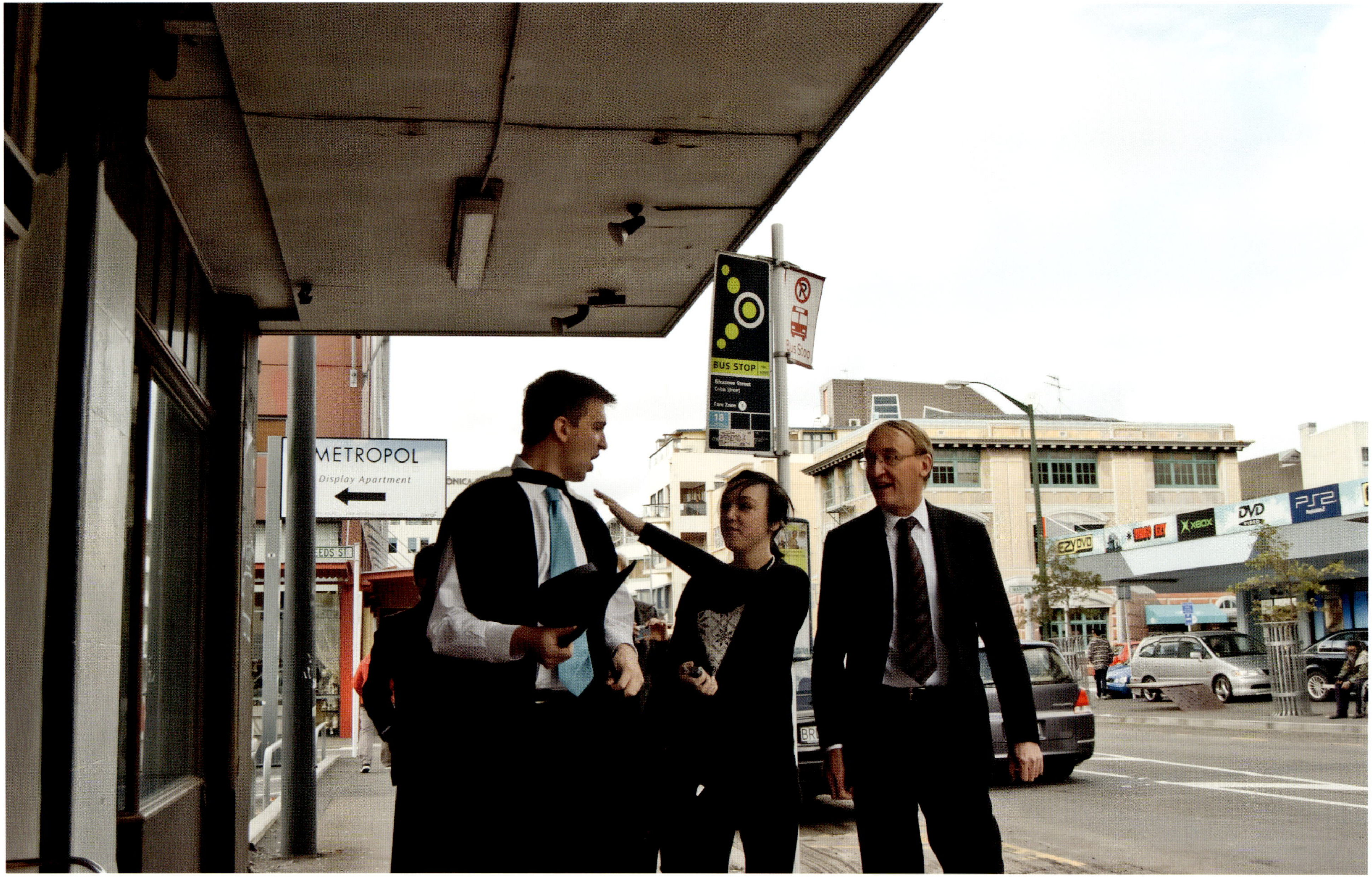
METROPOL
Display Apartment
BUS STOP
Bus Stop
XBOX
DVD

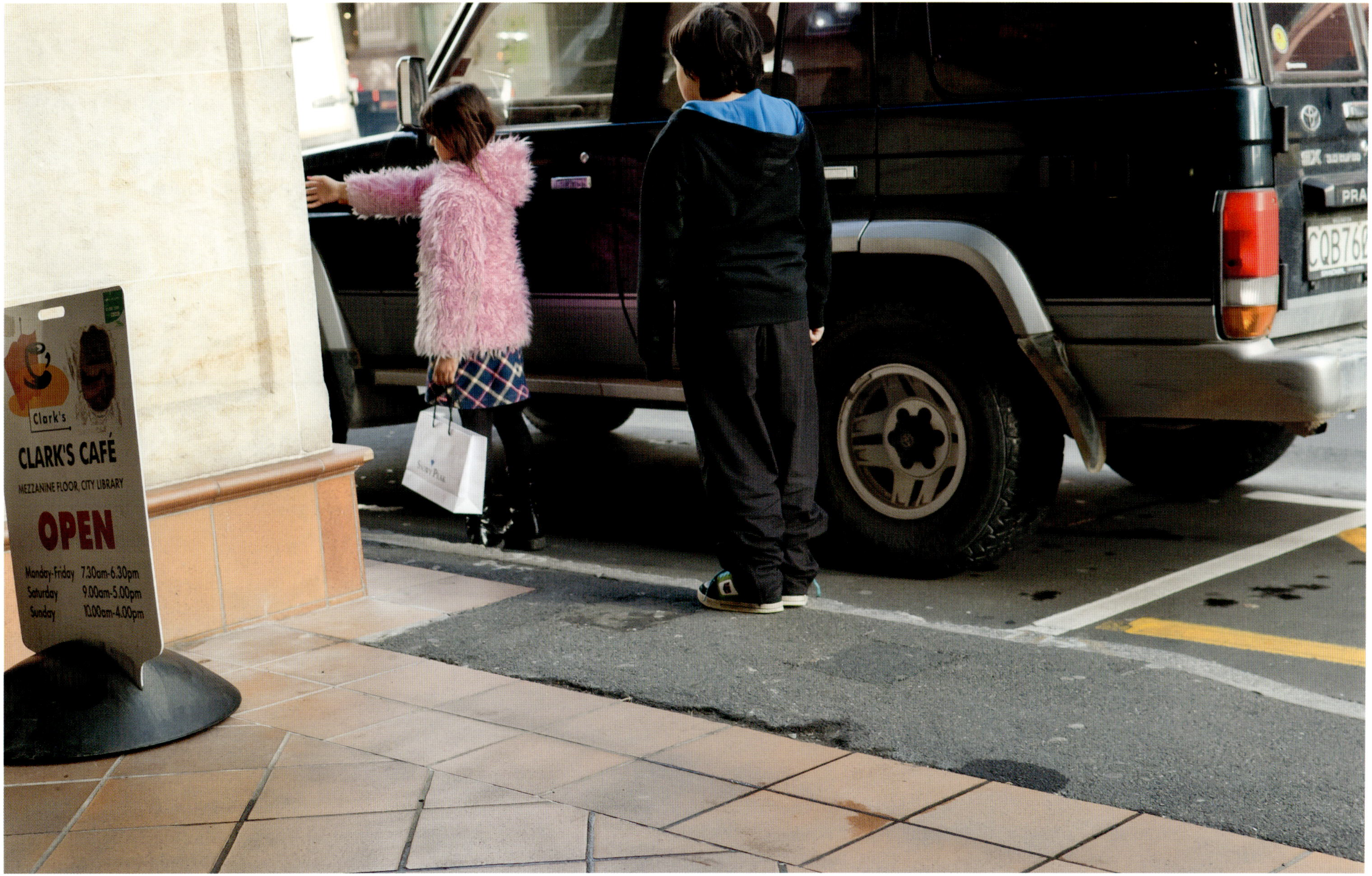
Clark's
CLARK'S CAFÉ
MEZZANINE FLOOR, CITY LIBRARY
OPEN
Monday-Friday 7.30am-6.30pm
Saturday 9.00am-5.00pm
Sunday 10.00am-4.00pm

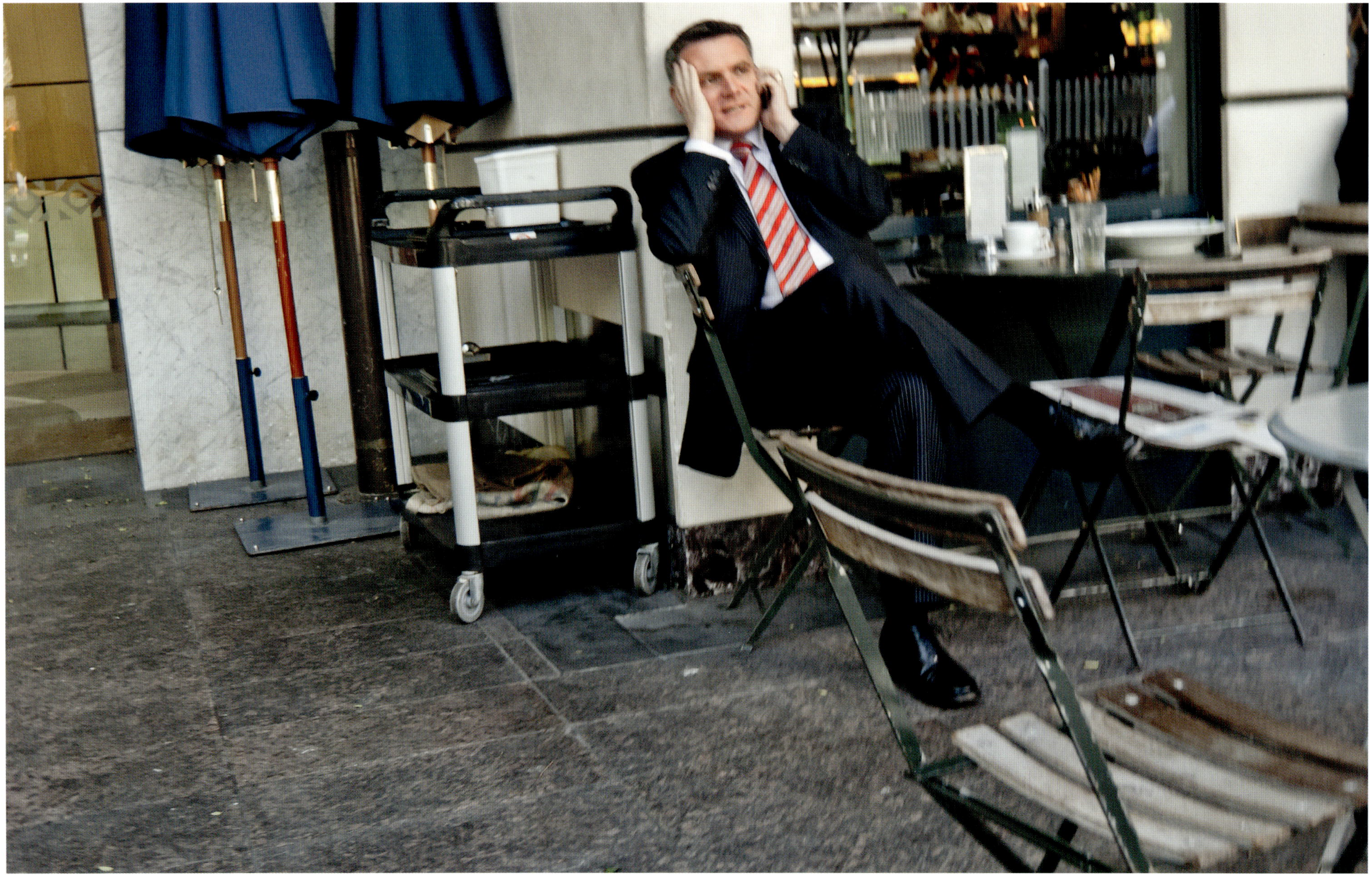

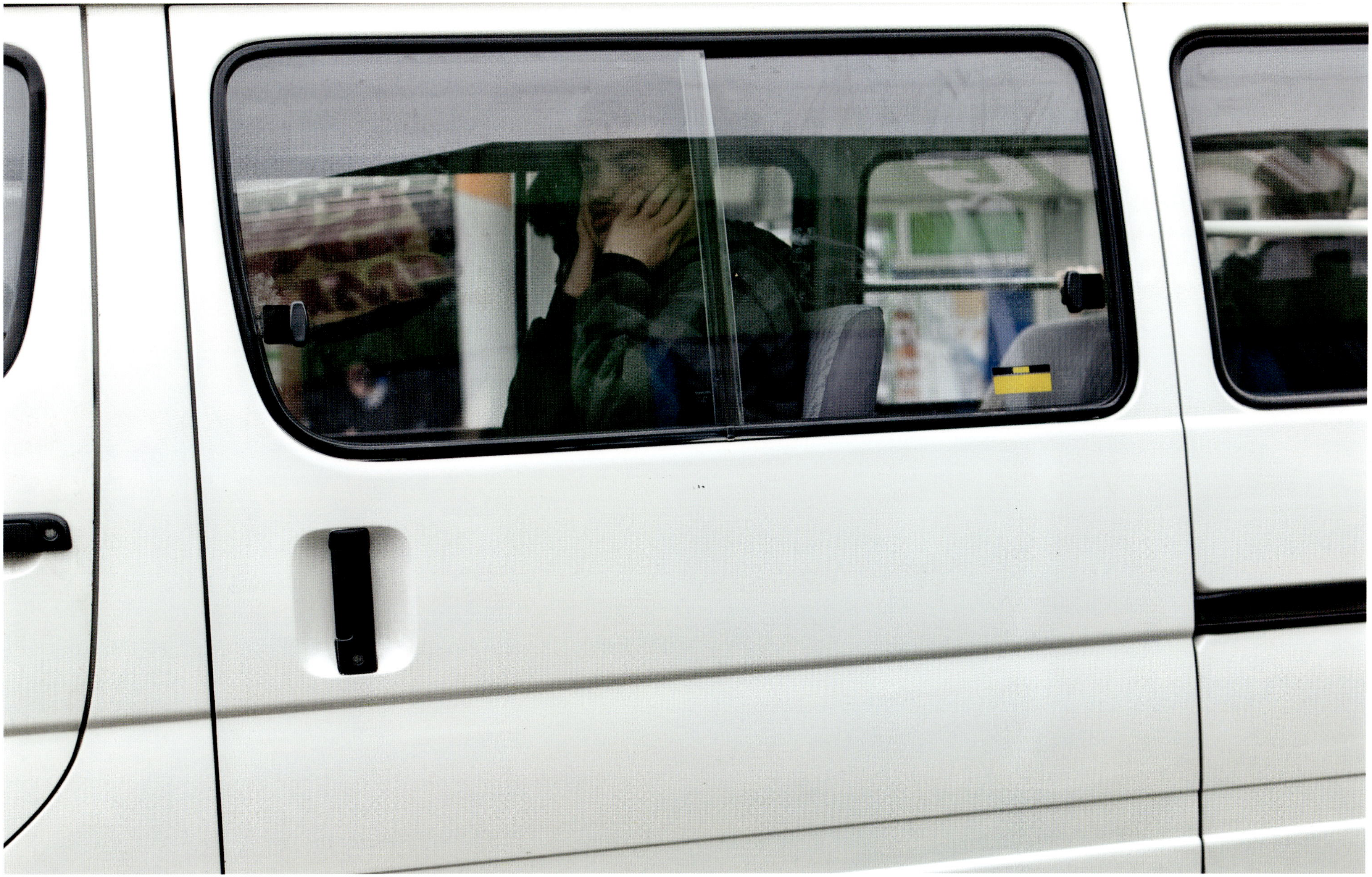

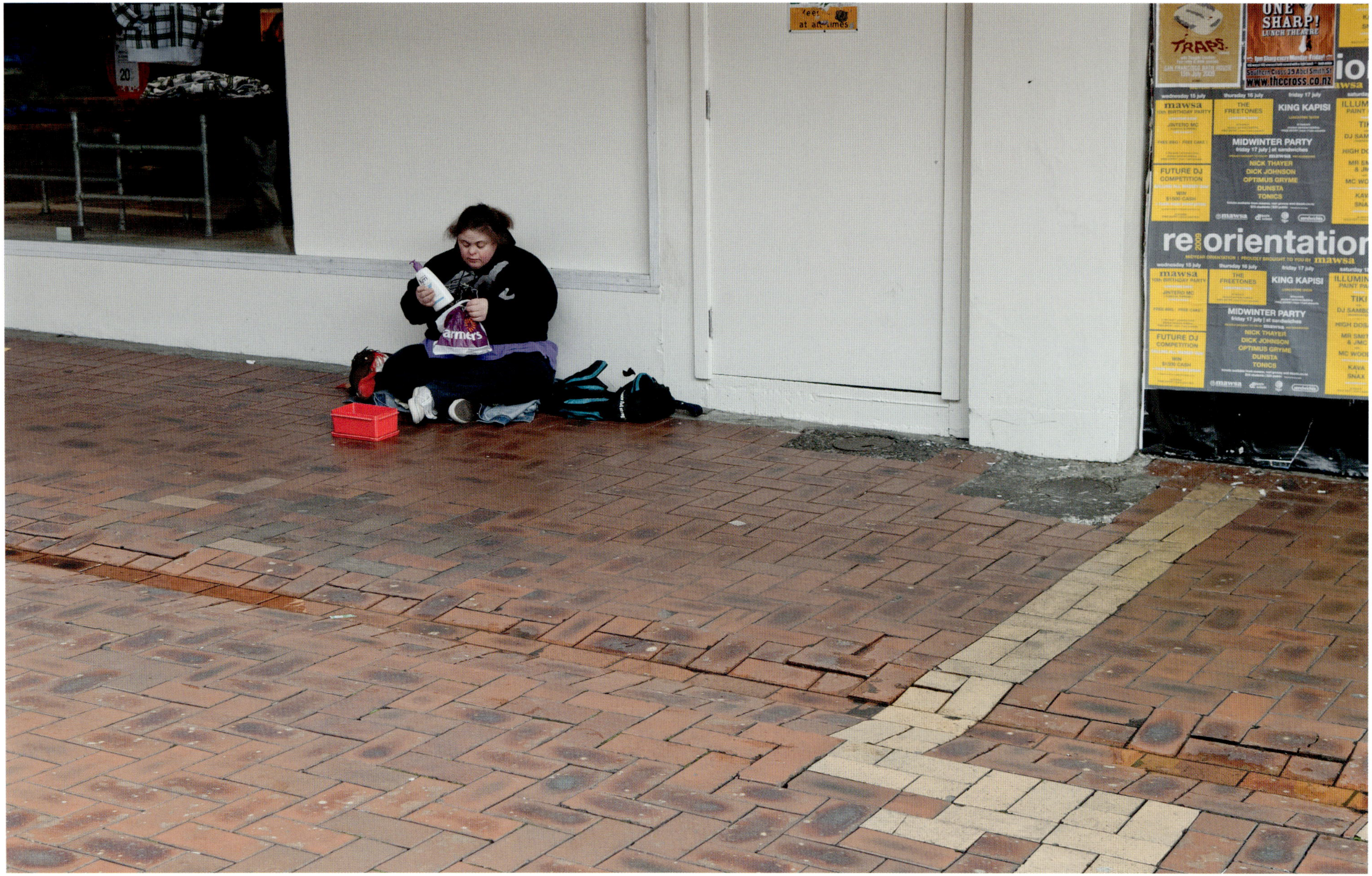
ONE SHARP!
LUNCH THEATRE
www.thecross.co.nz
re:orientation
mawsa
THE FREETONES
KING KAPISI
MIDWINTER PARTY
NICK THAYER
DICK JOHNSON
OPTIMUS GRYME
DUNSTA
TONICS
FUTURE DJ COMPETITION

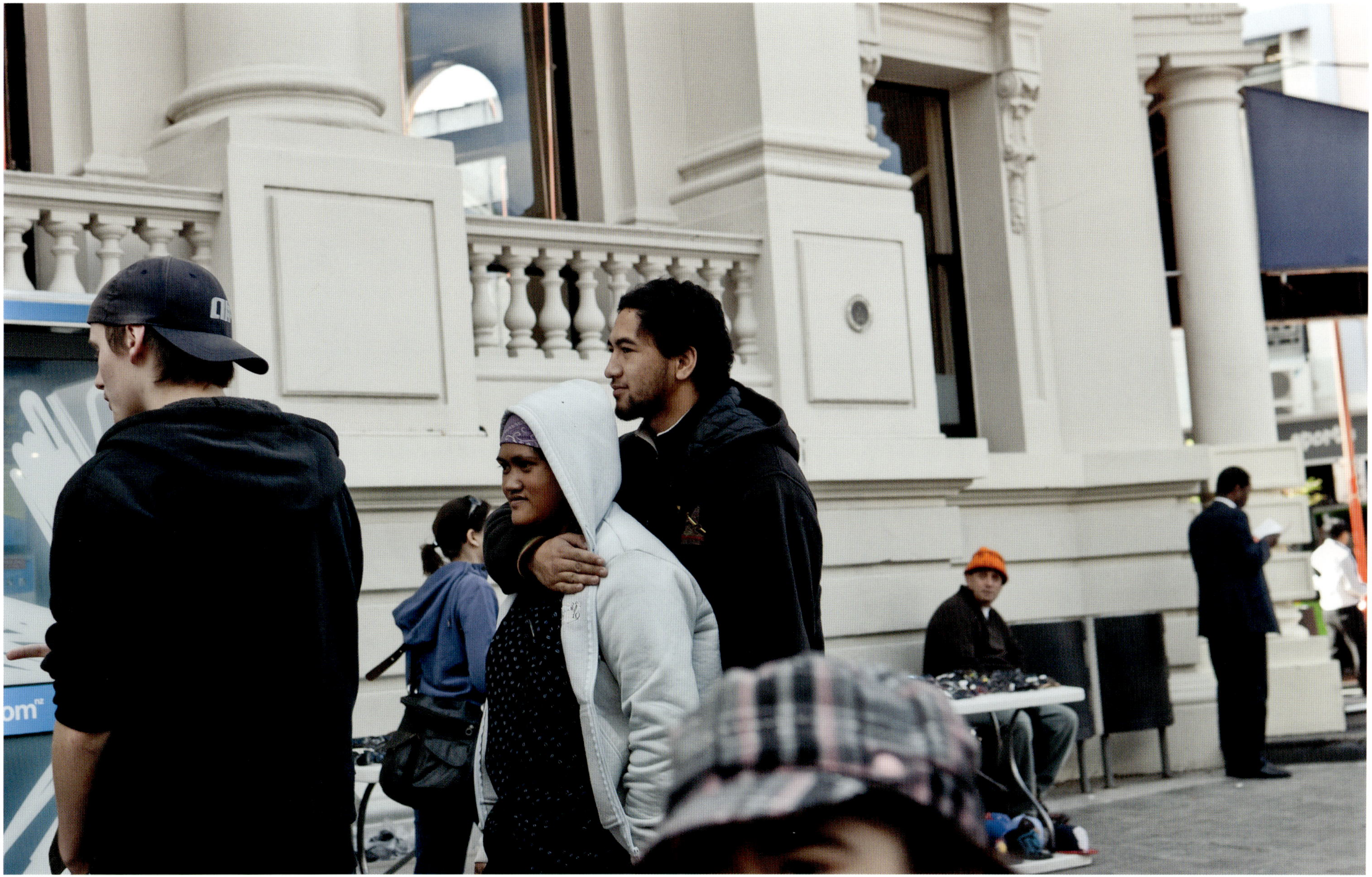

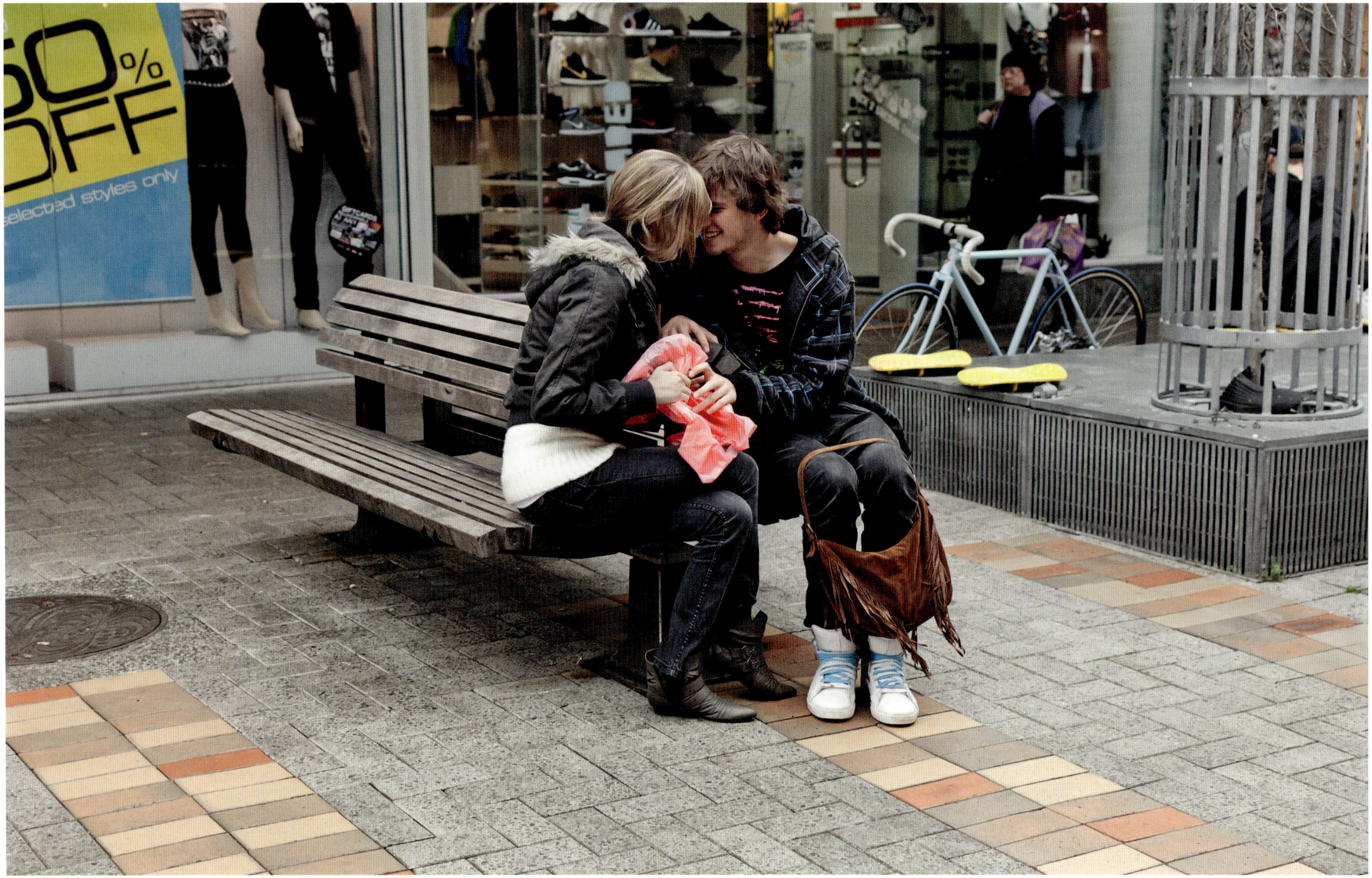
60% OFF
selected styles only

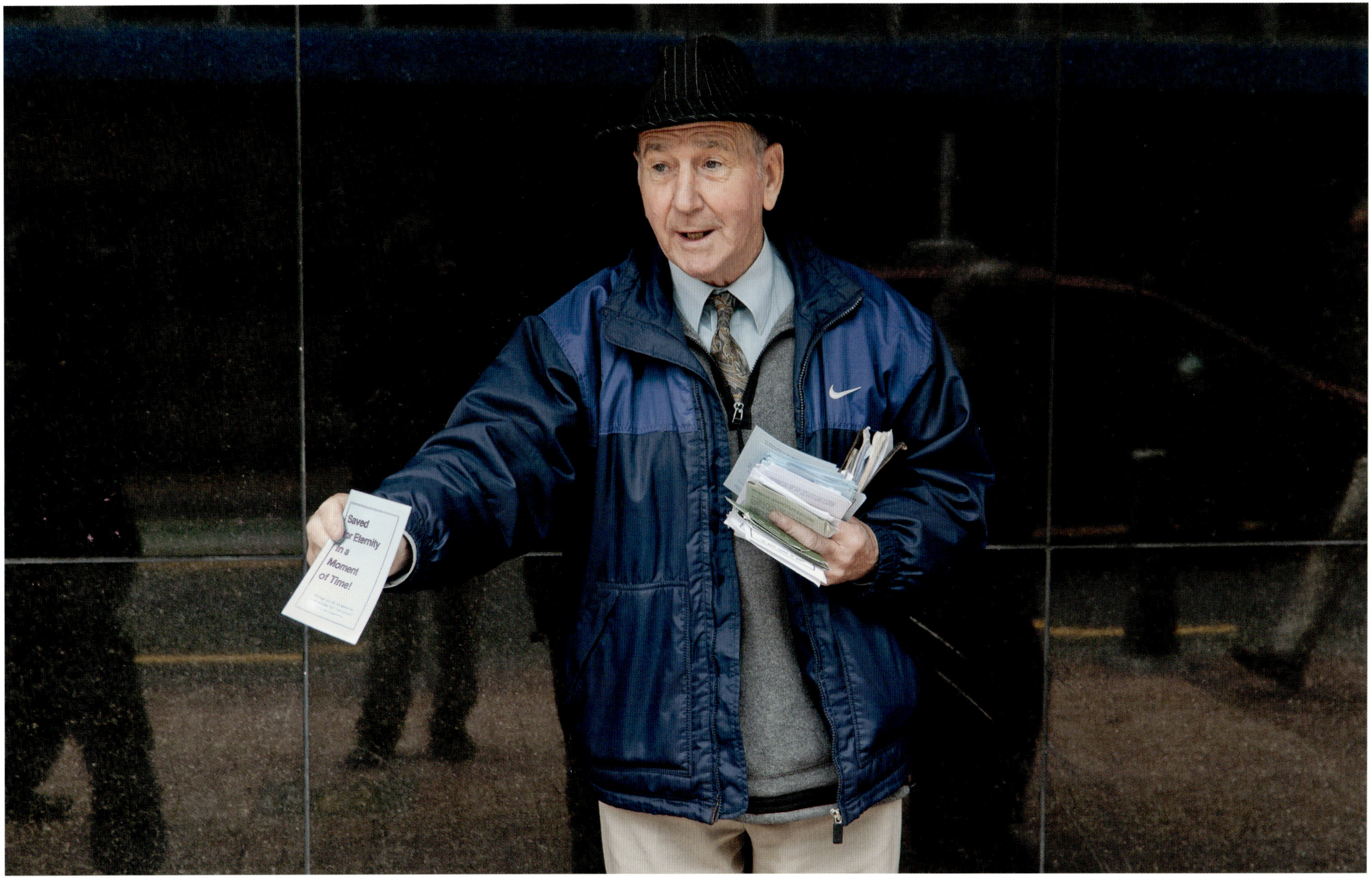
Saved
or Eternity
in a
Moment
of Time!

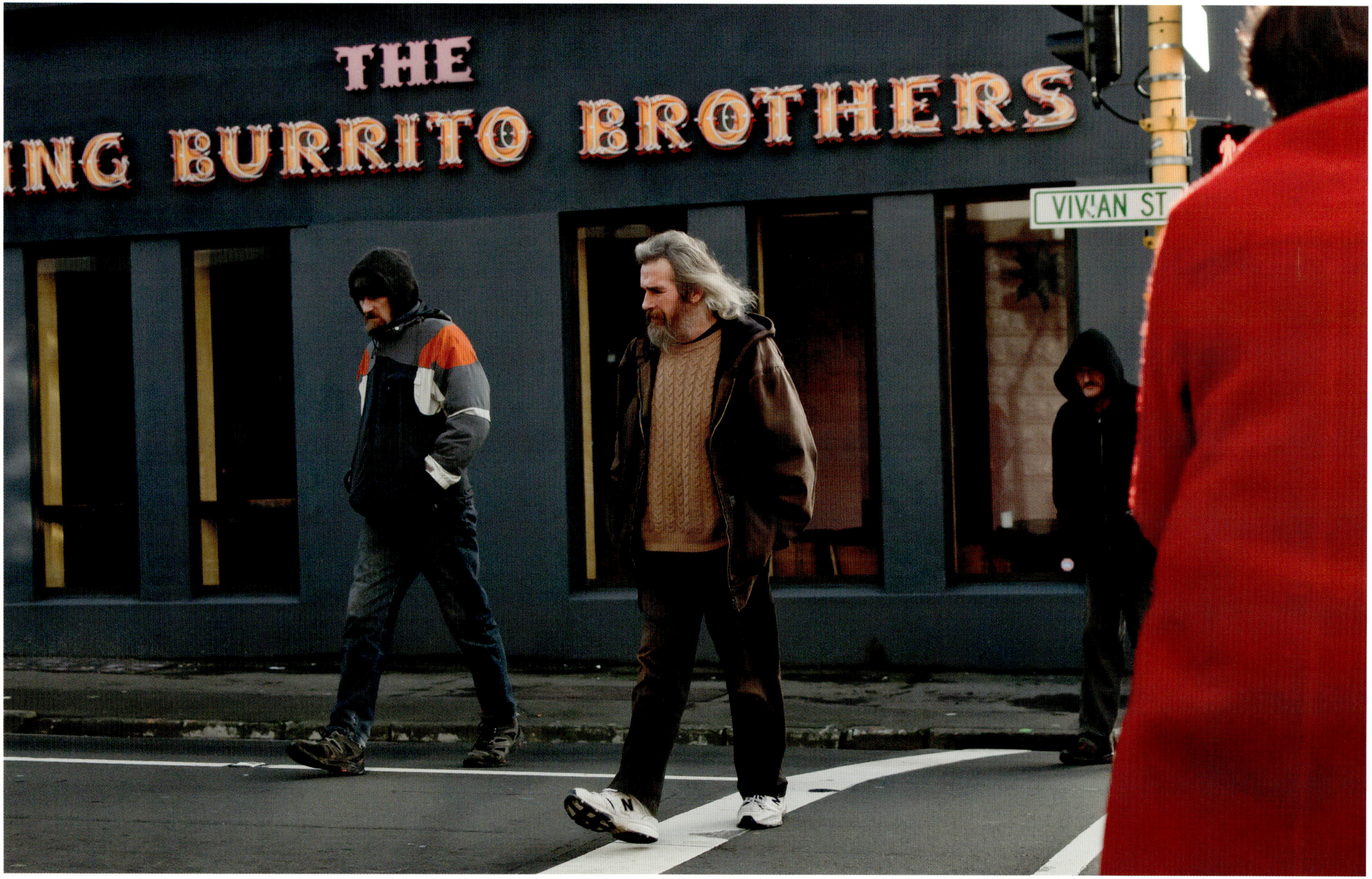
THE
NG BURRITO BROTHERS
VIVIAN ST

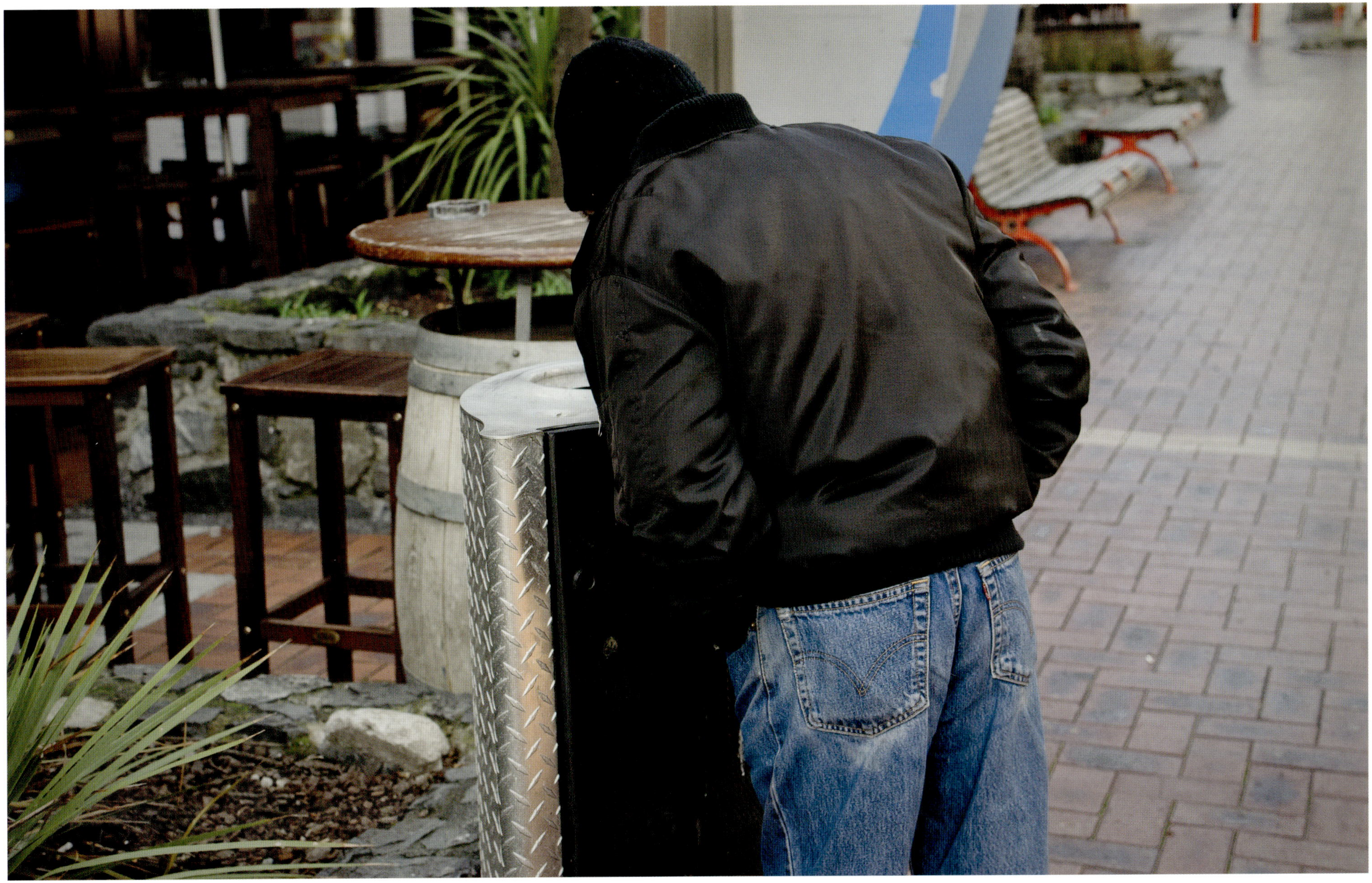

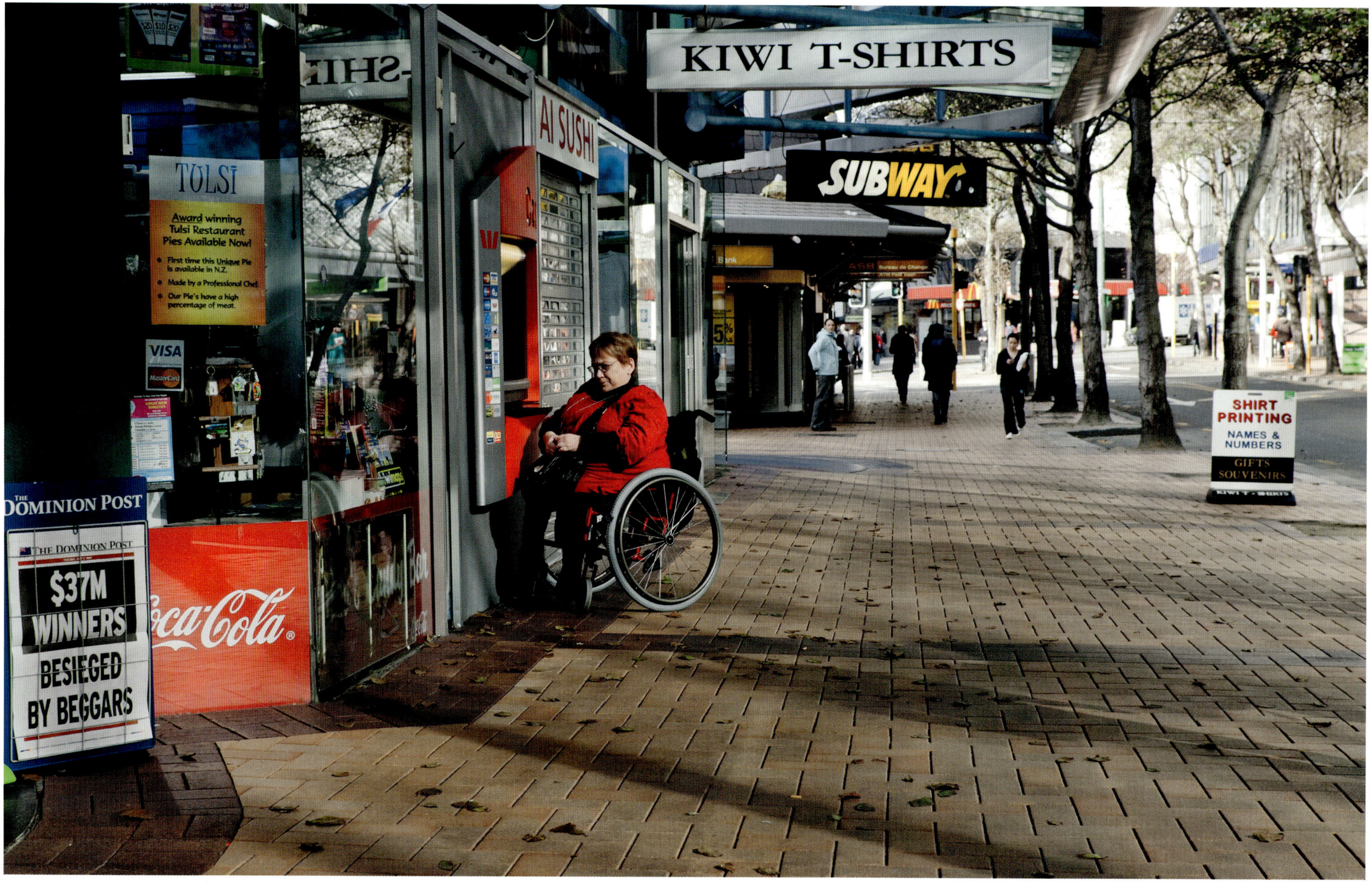
KIWI T-SHIRTS
SUBWAY
AI SUSHI
TULSI
Award winning Tulsi Restaurant Pies Available Now!
First time this Unique Pie is available in N.Z.
Made by a Professional Chef.
Our Pie's have a high percentage of meat.
VISA
MasterCard
THE DOMINION POST
$37M WINNERS BESIEGED BY BEGGARS
SHIRT PRINTING
NAMES & NUMBERS
GIFTS SOUVENIRS

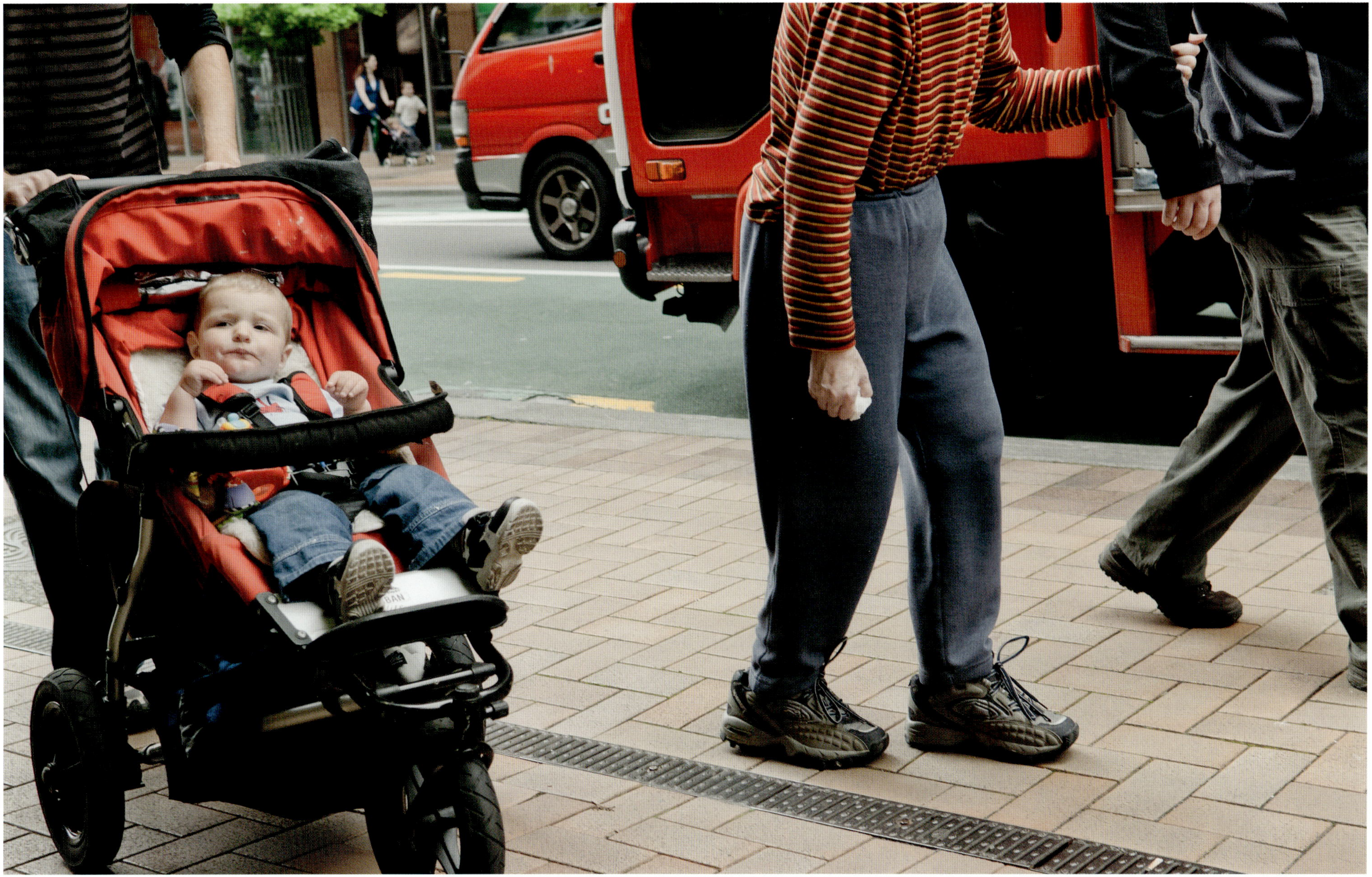

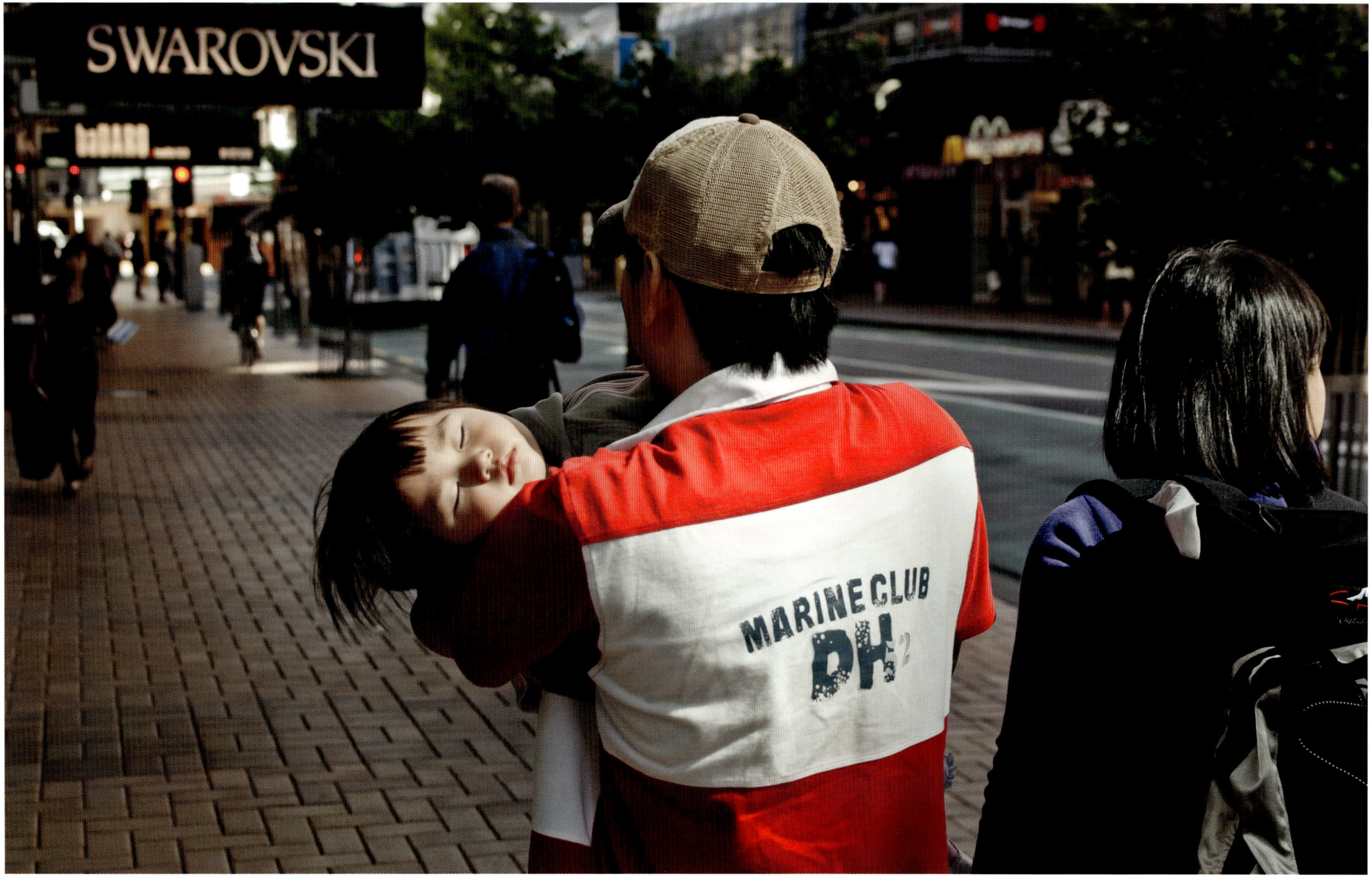
SWAROVSKI
MARINE CLUB
PH2

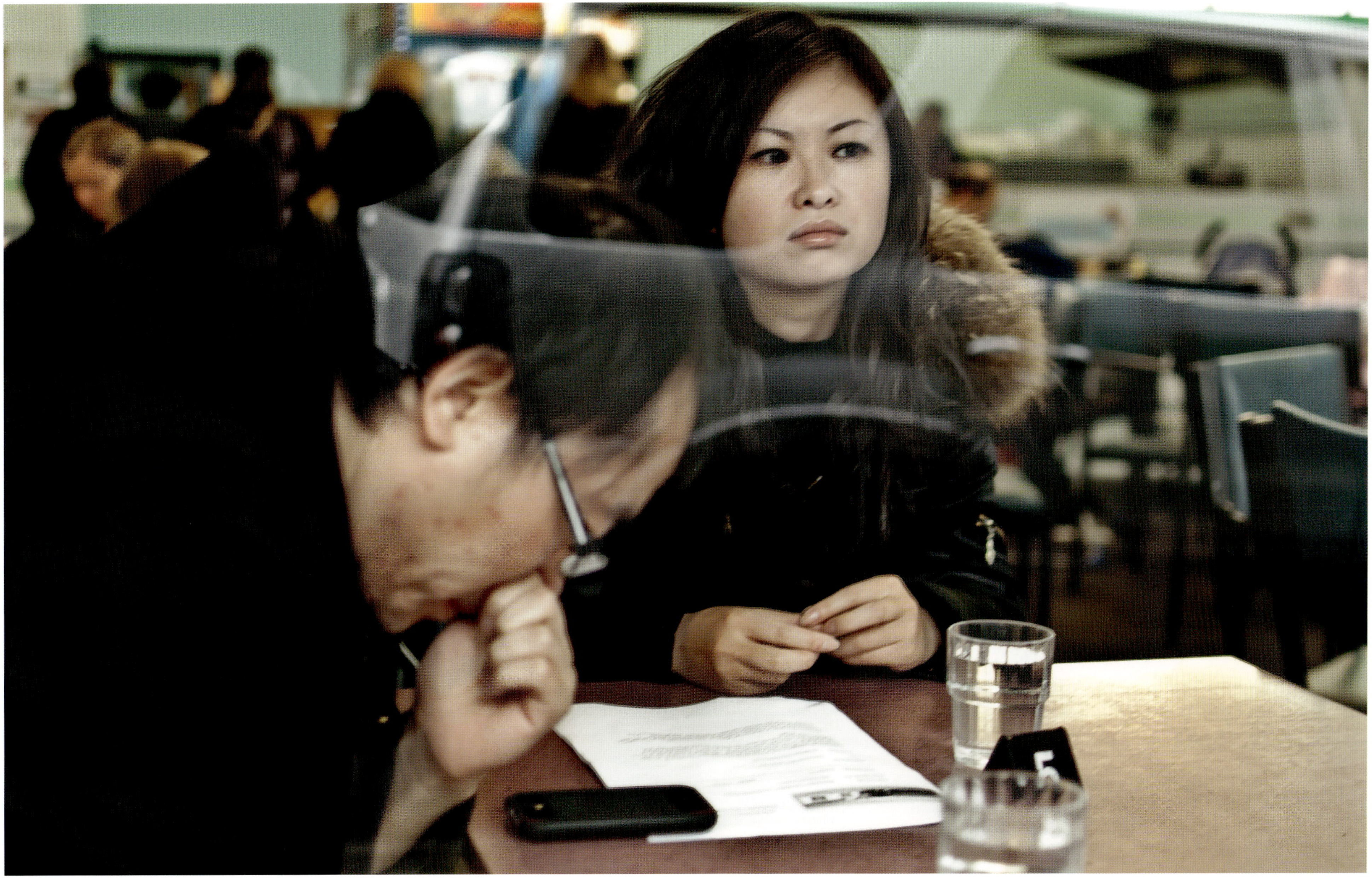

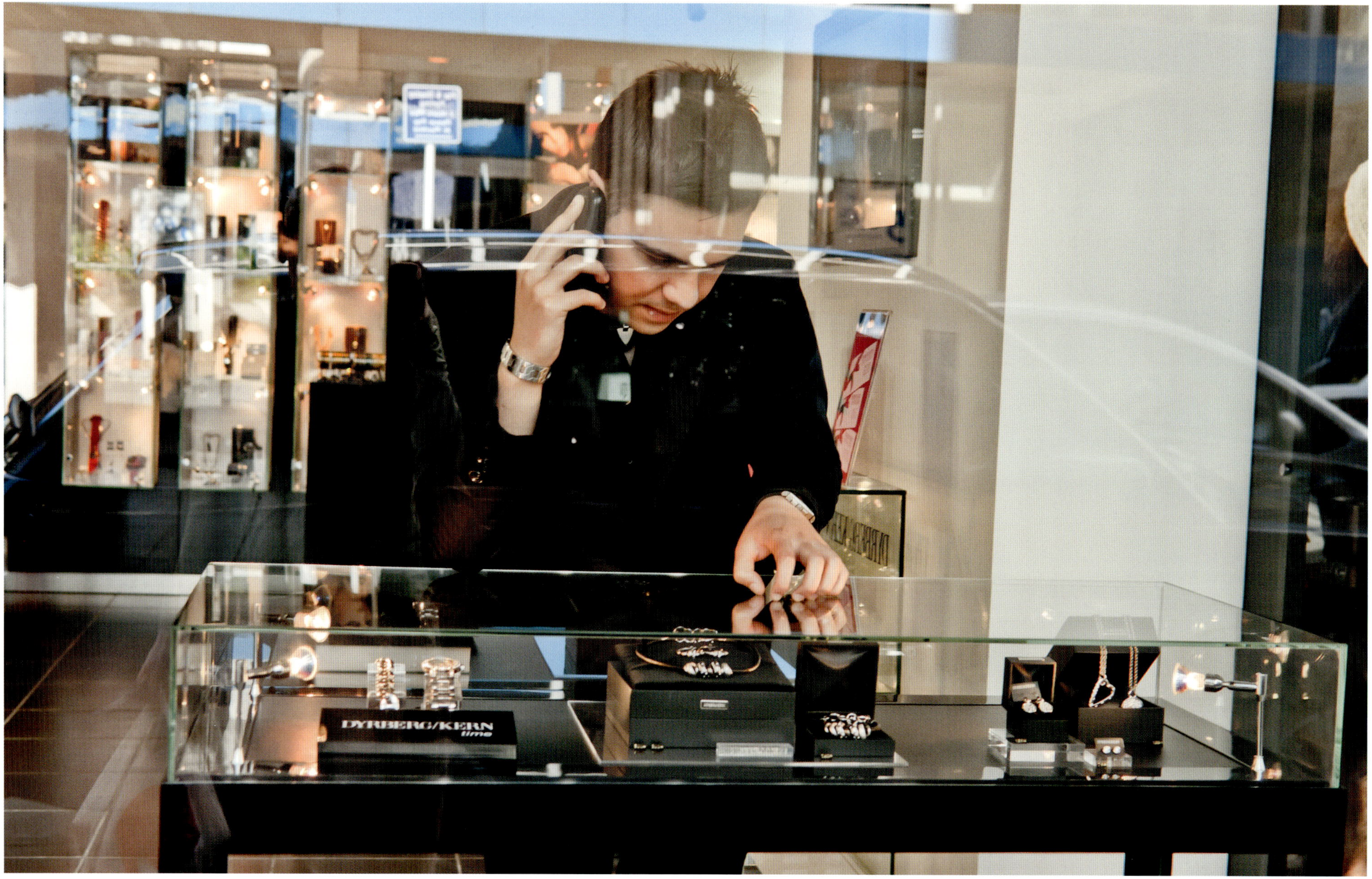
DYRBERG/KERN
time

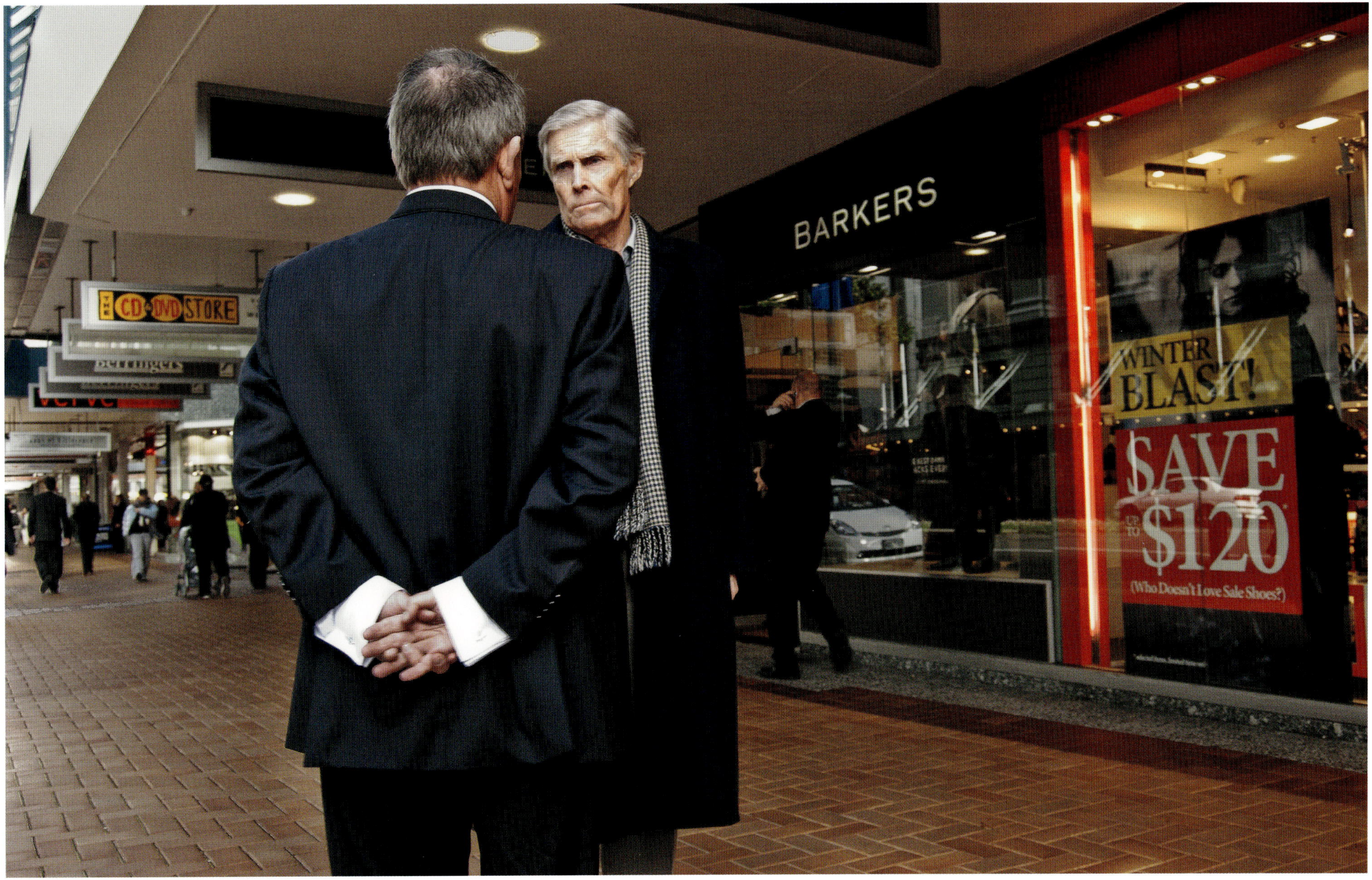
BARKERS
WINTER BLAST!
SAVE
UP TO $120*
(Who Doesn't Love Sale Shoes?)
CD DVD STORE

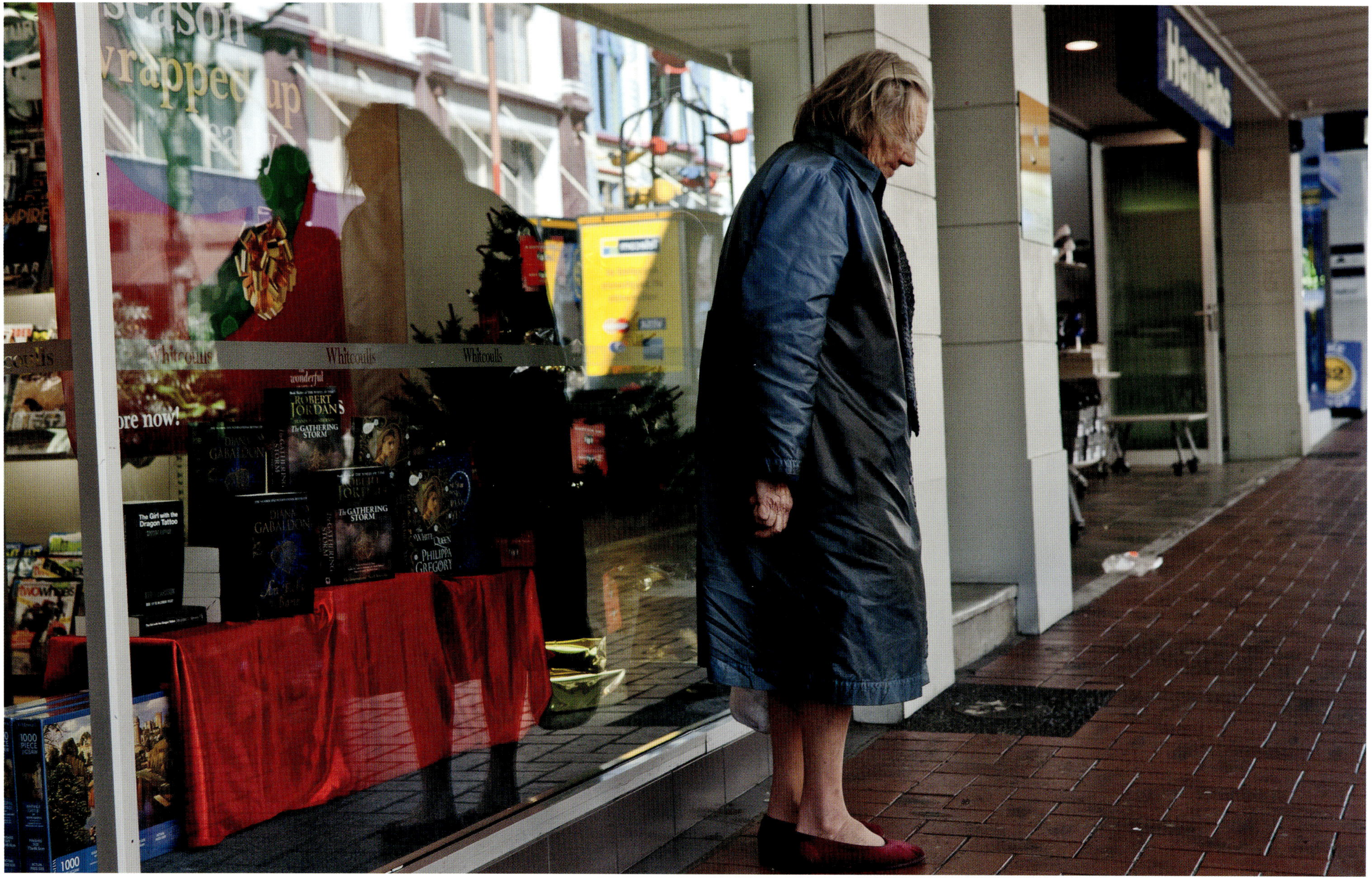

wrapped up
Whitcoulls
ore now!
ROBERT JORDAN'S
The GATHERING STORM
DIANA GABALDON
The Girl with the Dragon Tattoo
WHITE QUEEN
PHILIPPA GREGORY
1000 PIECE JIGSAW

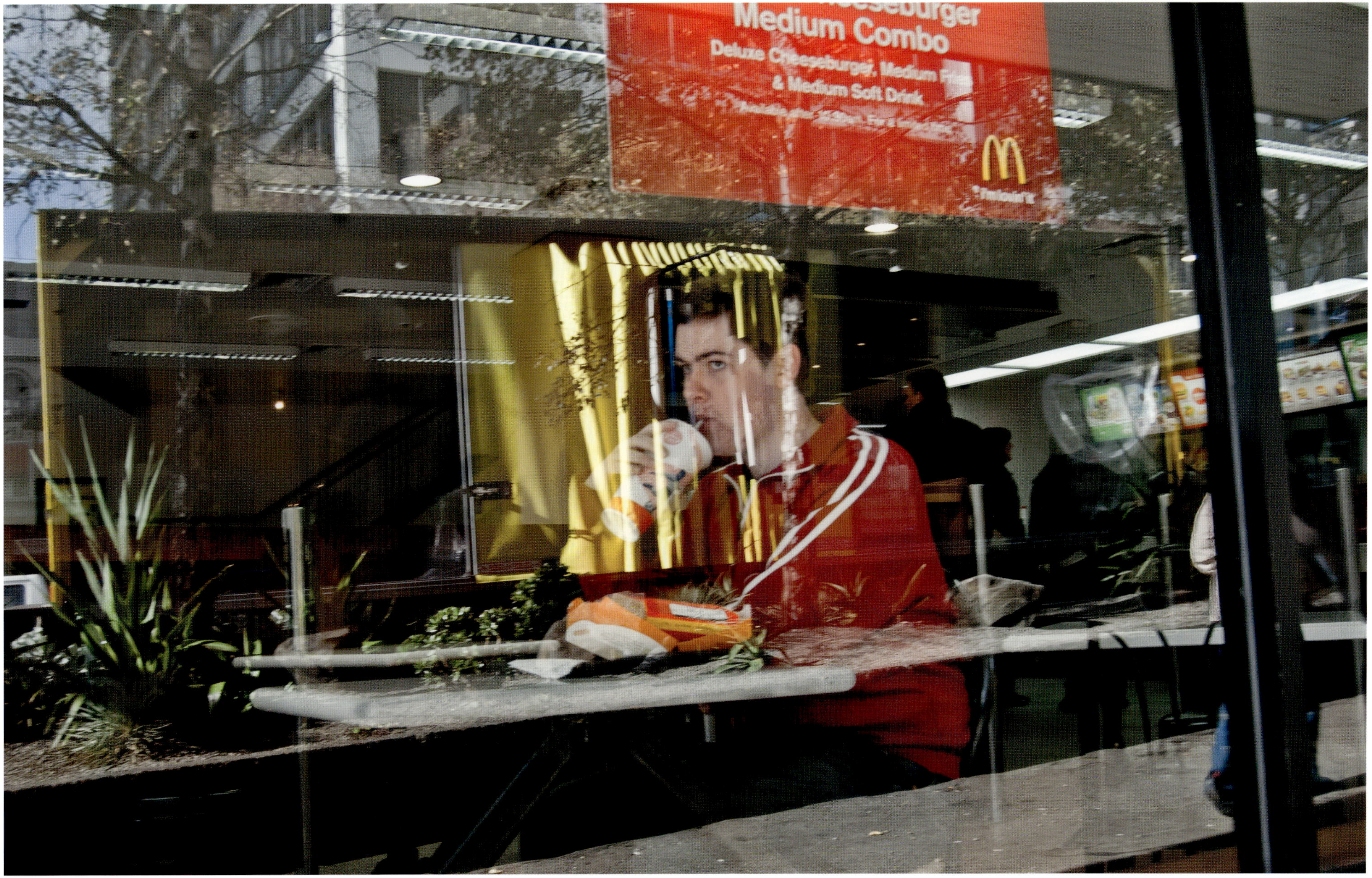
Medium Combo
Deluxe Cheeseburger, Medium
& Medium Soft Drink.

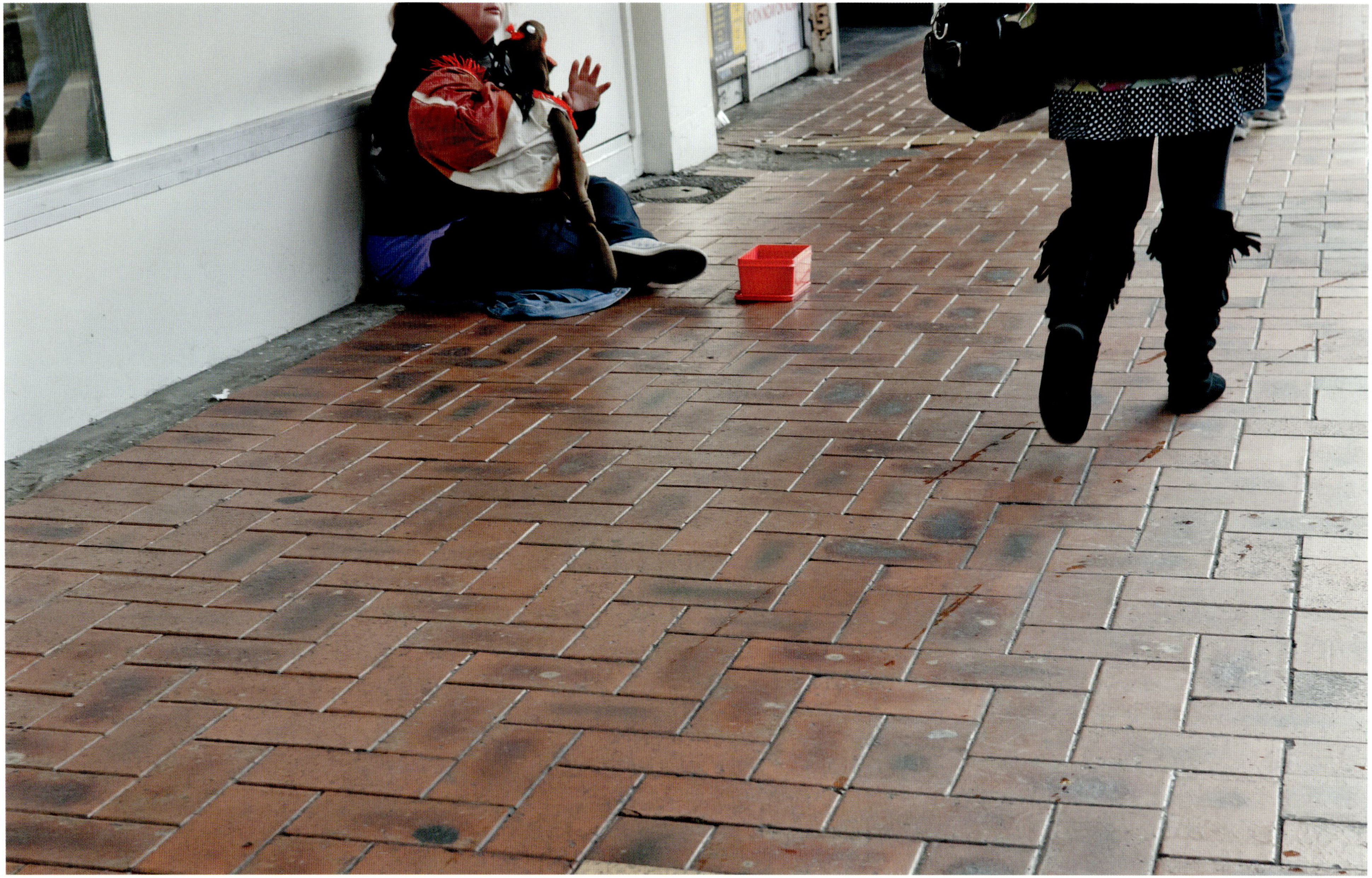

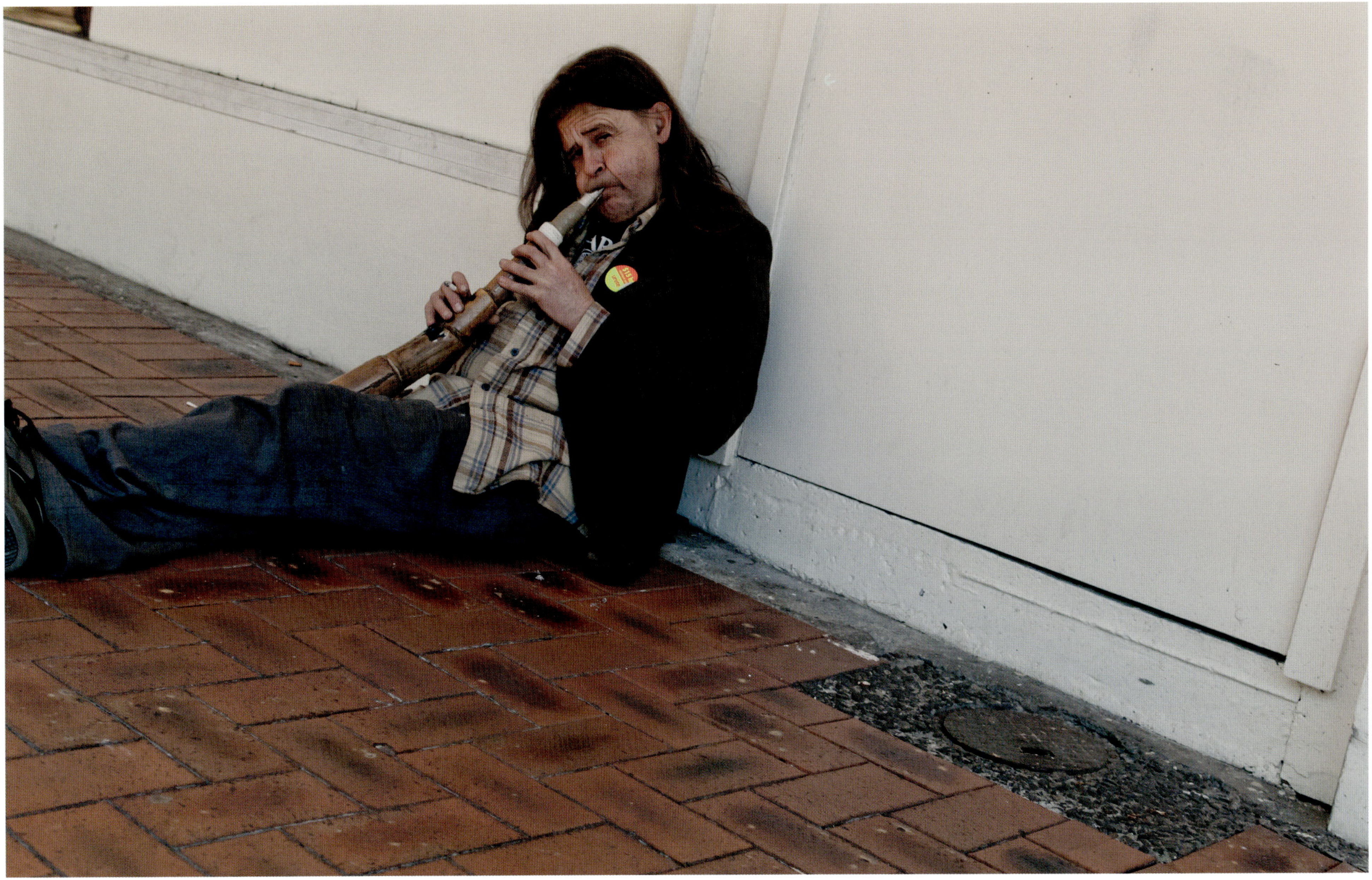

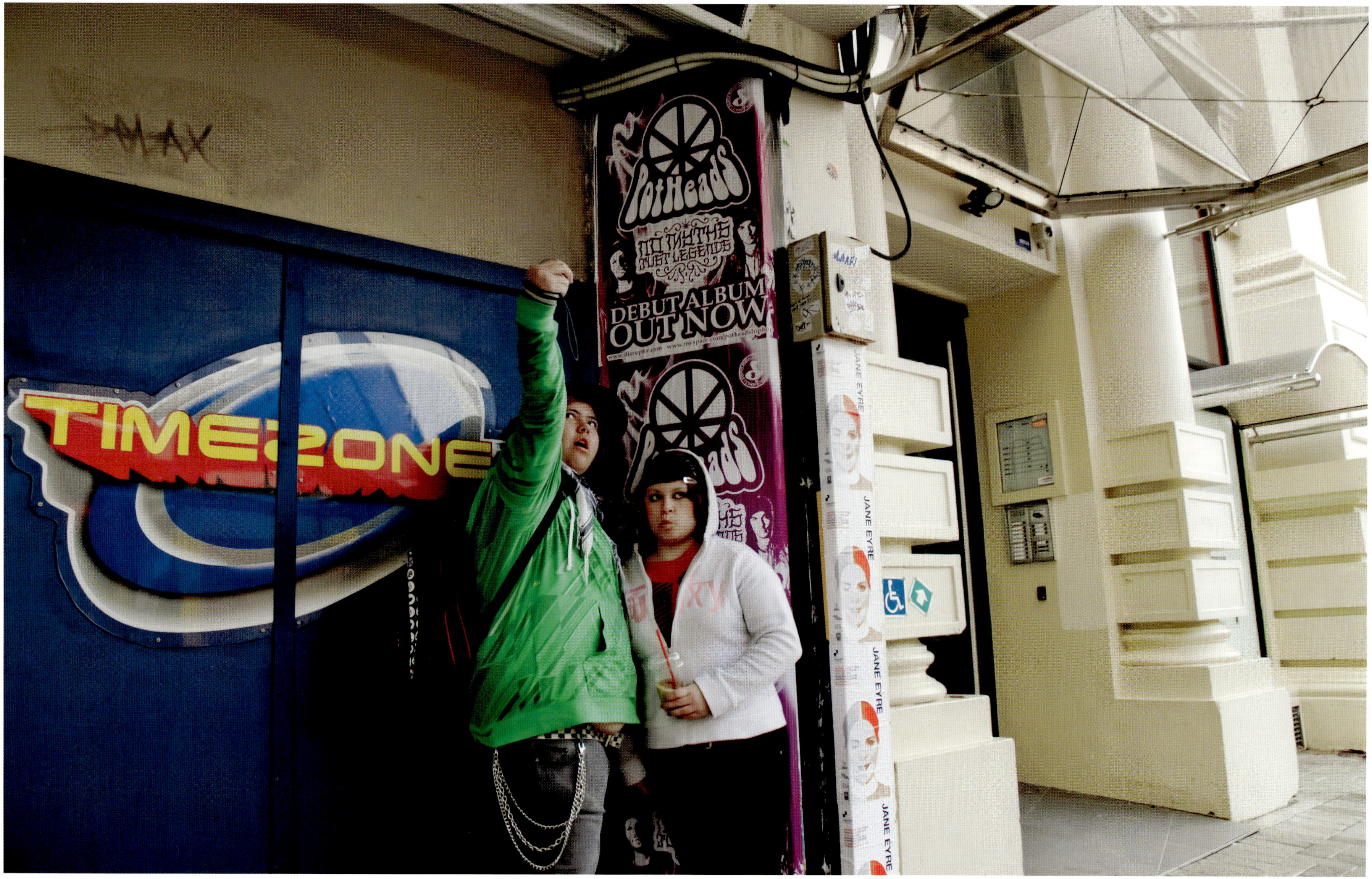
TIMEZONE
PotHeads
NO MYTHS JUST LEGENDS
DEBUT ALBUM
OUT NOW
JANE EYRE

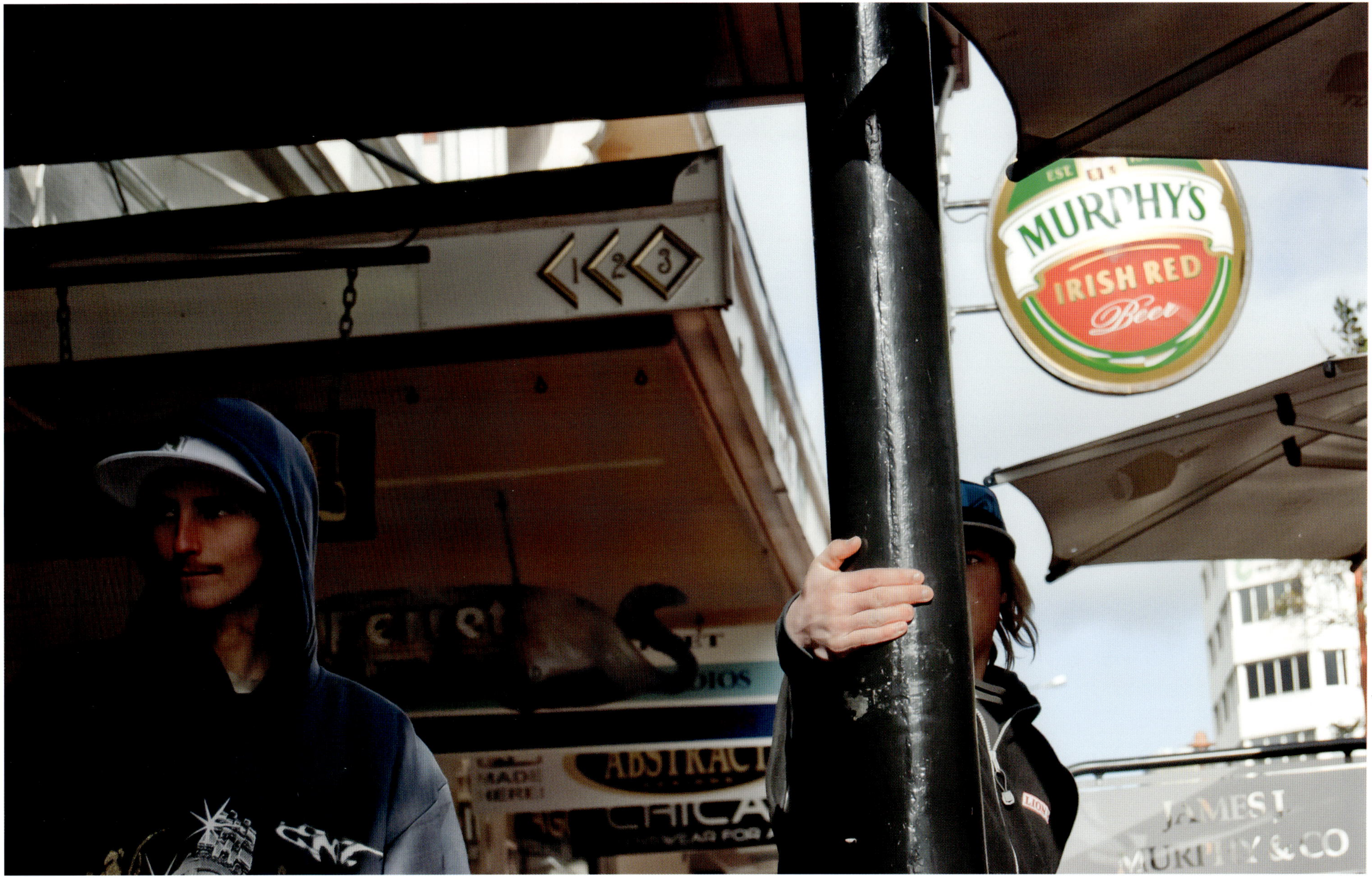
MURPHY'S
IRISH RED
Beer

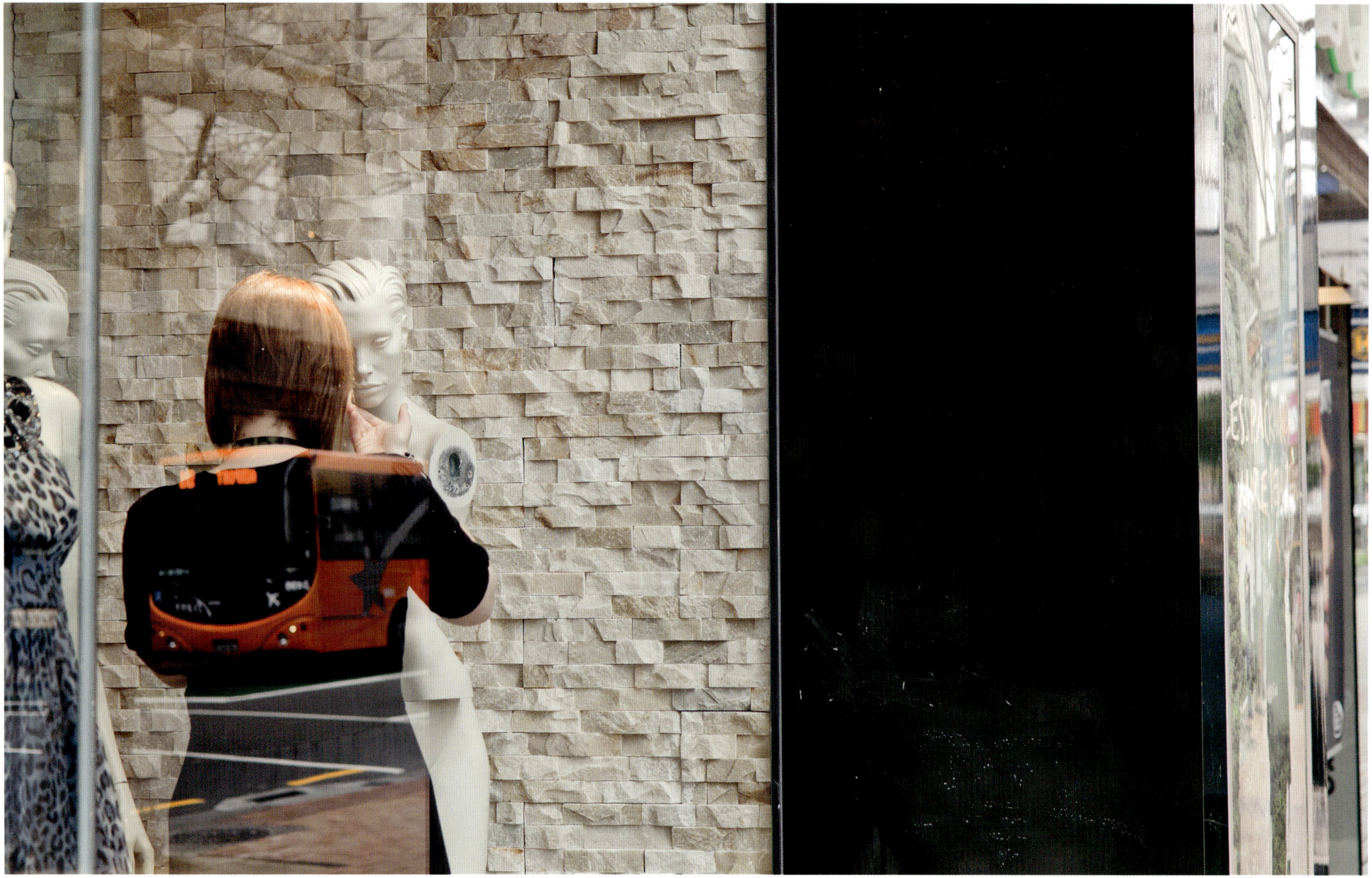

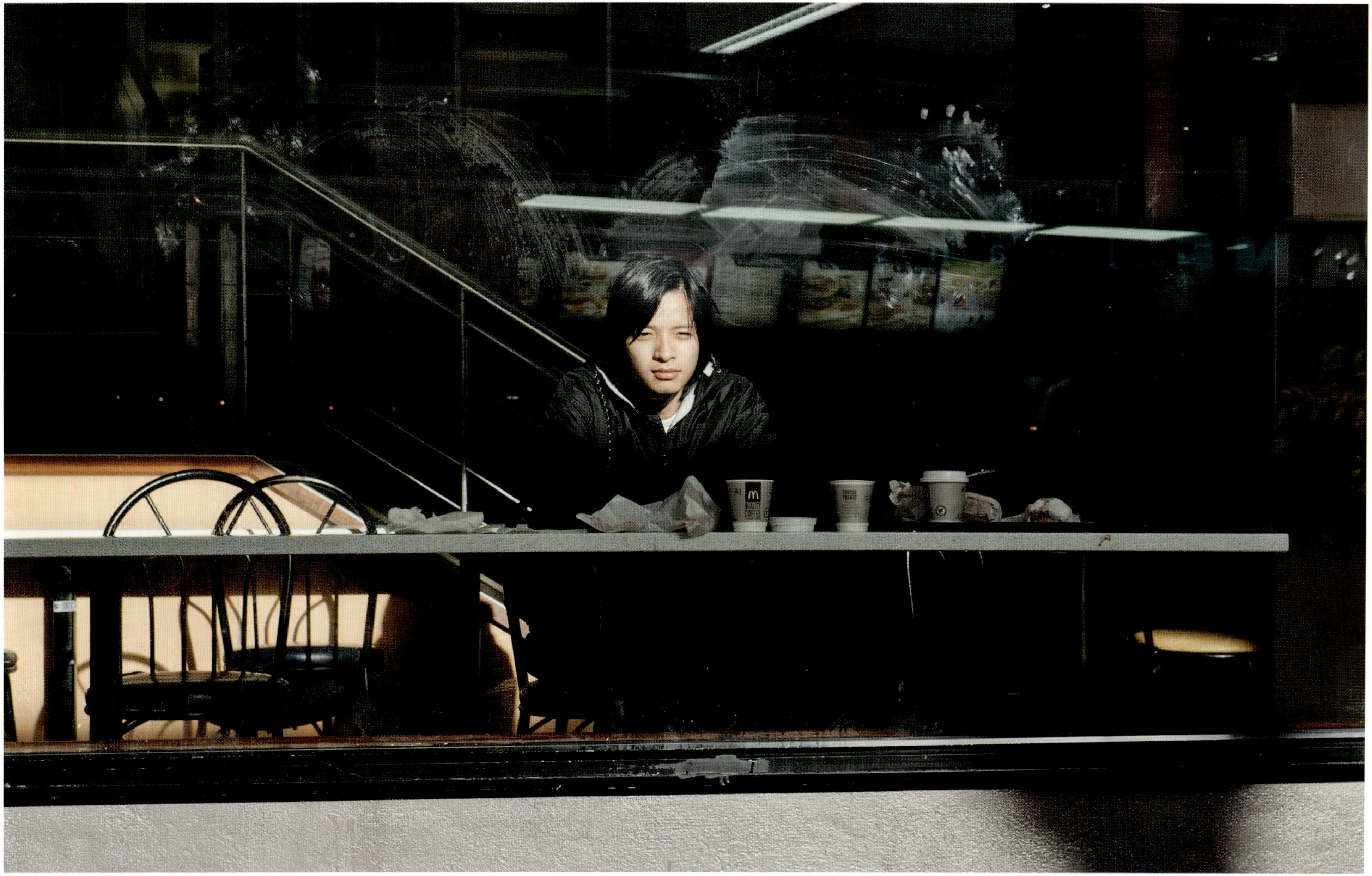

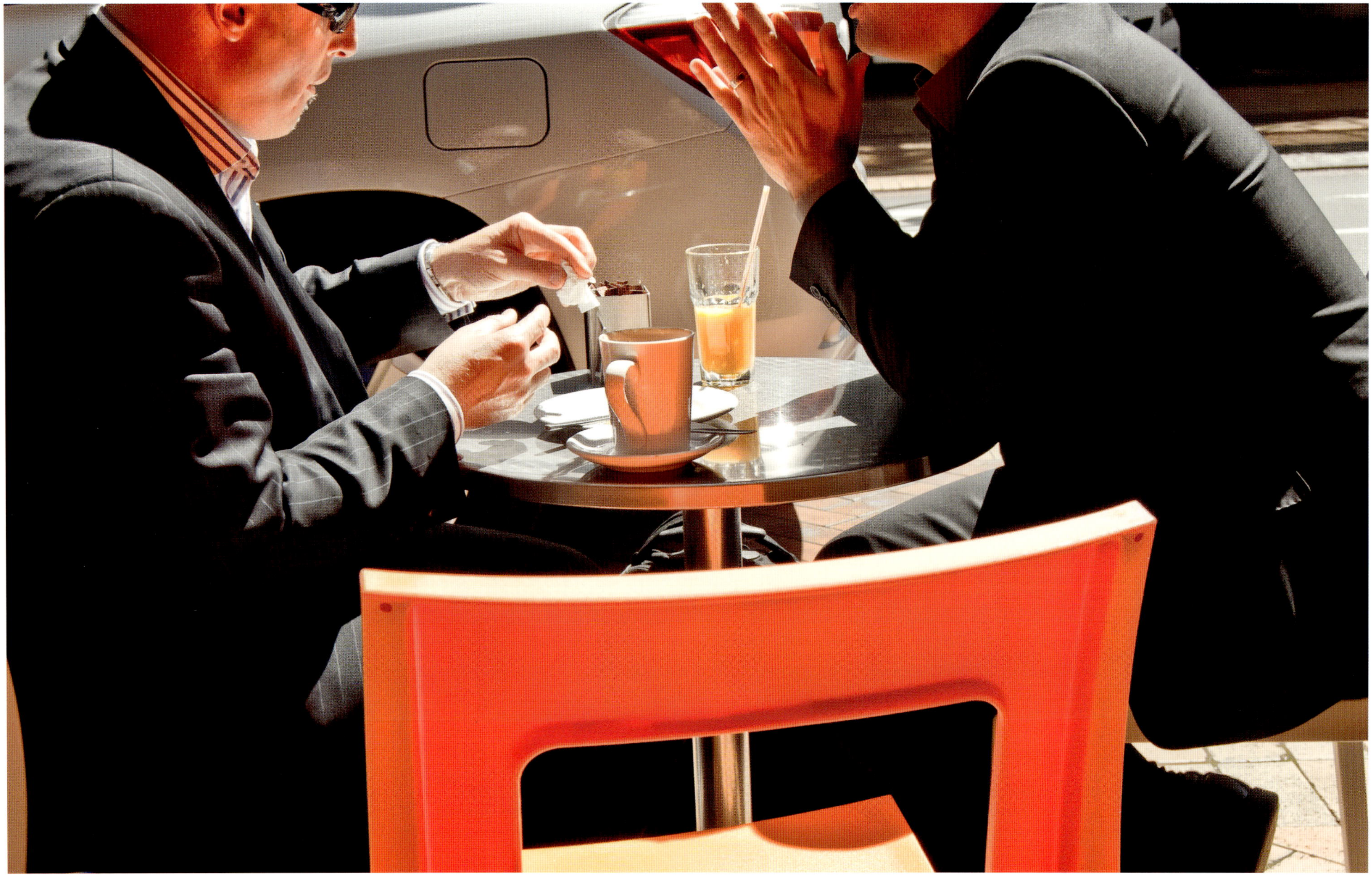

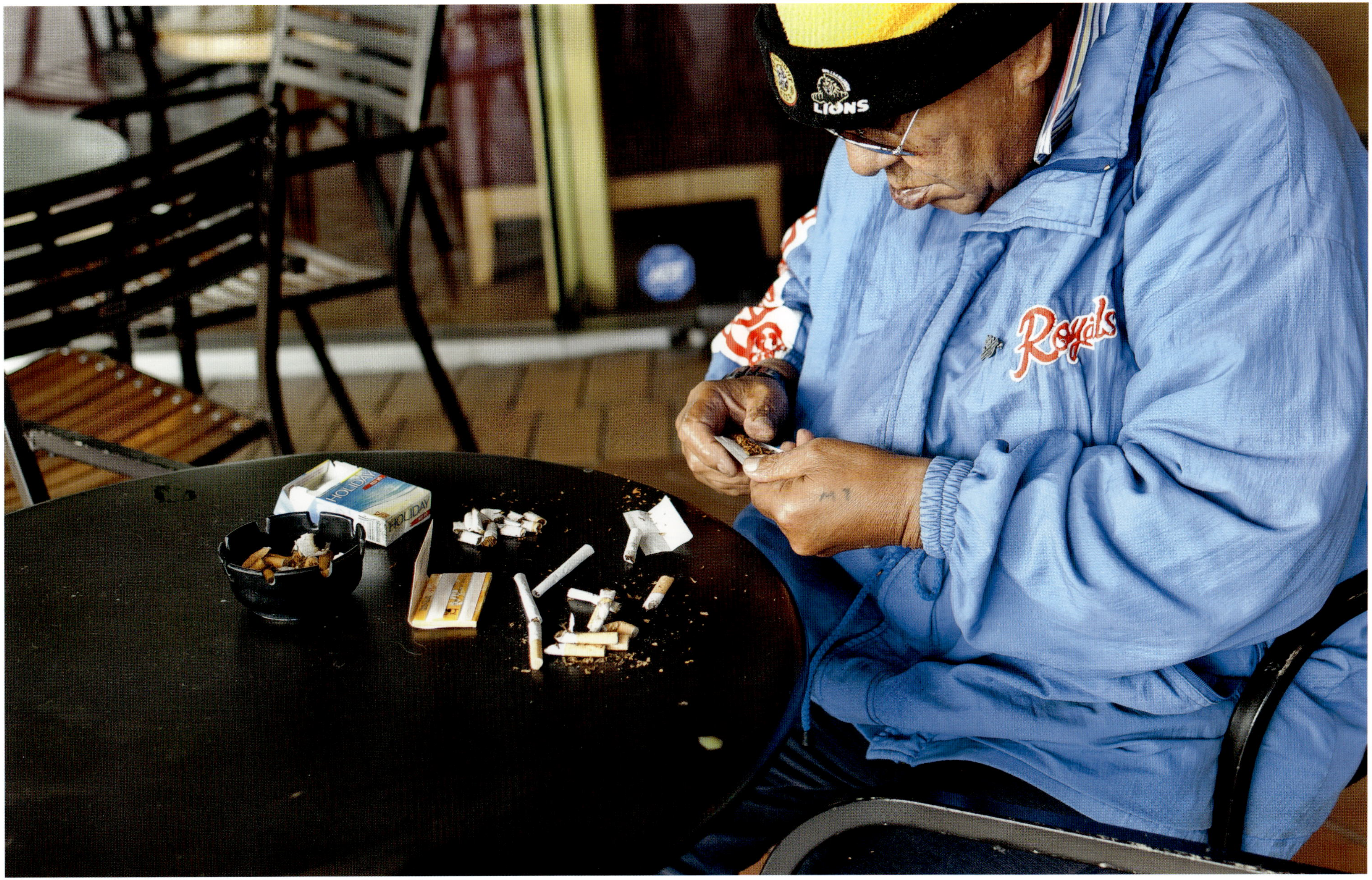
LIONS
Royals
HOLIDAY

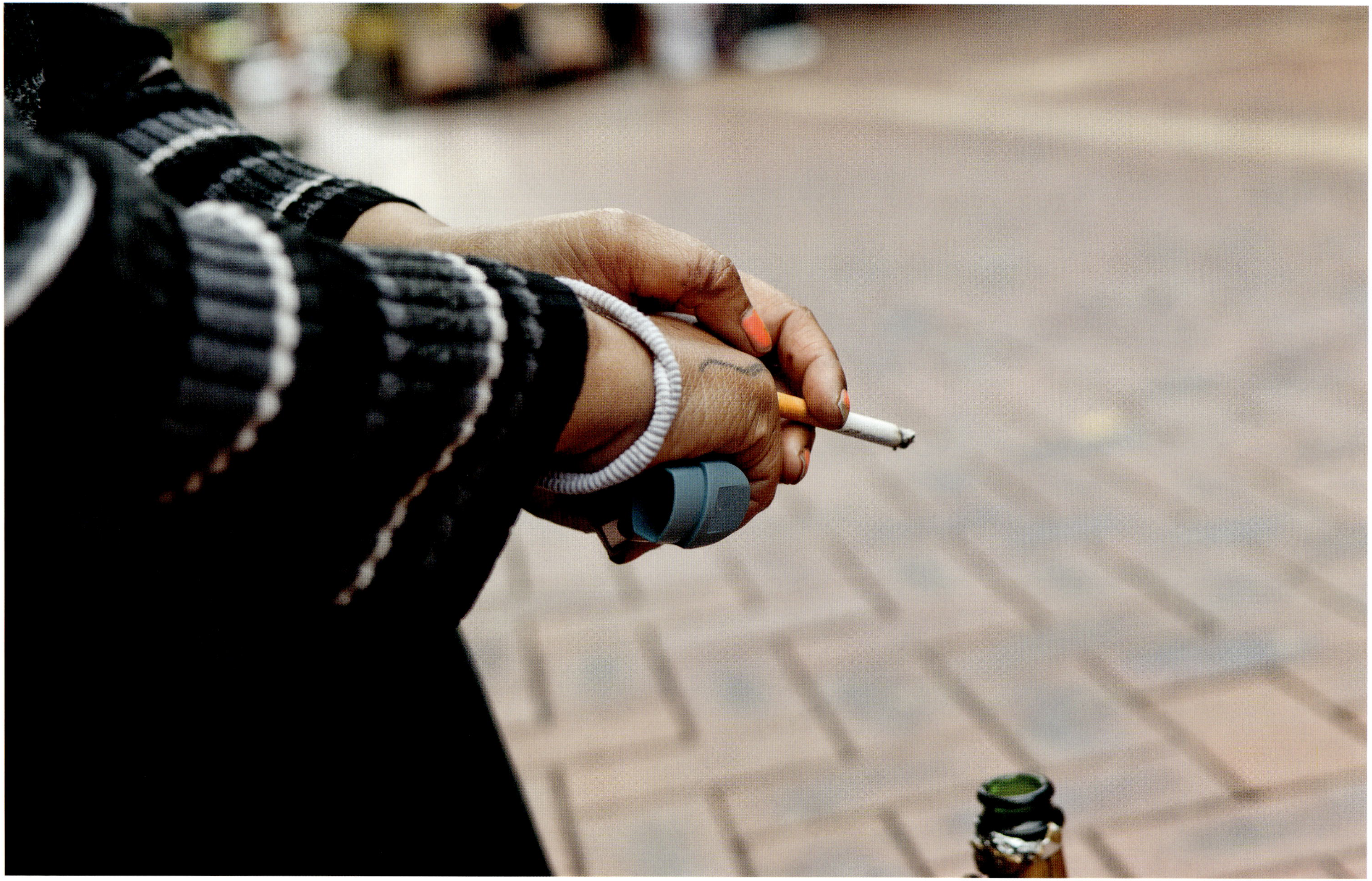

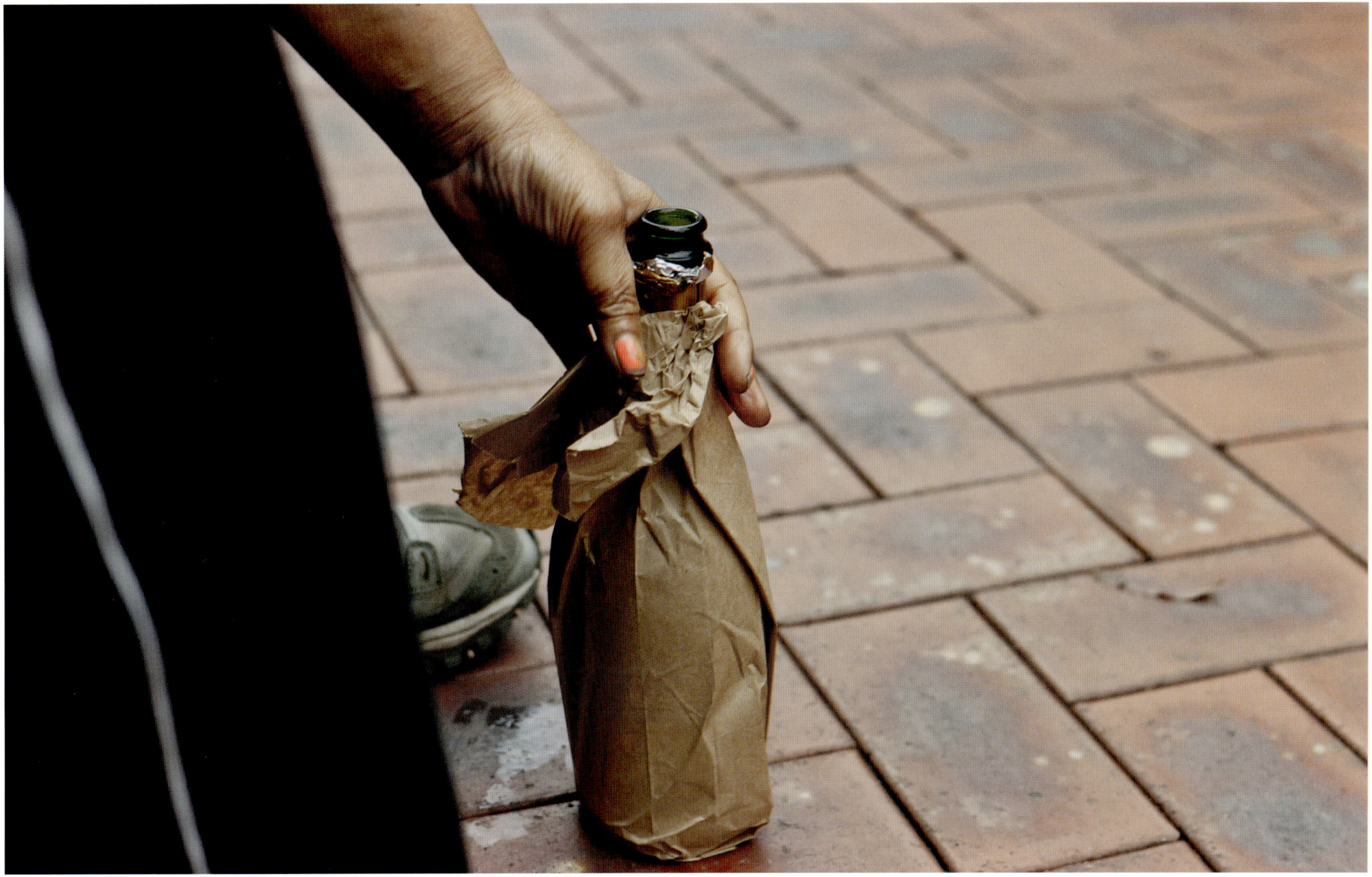

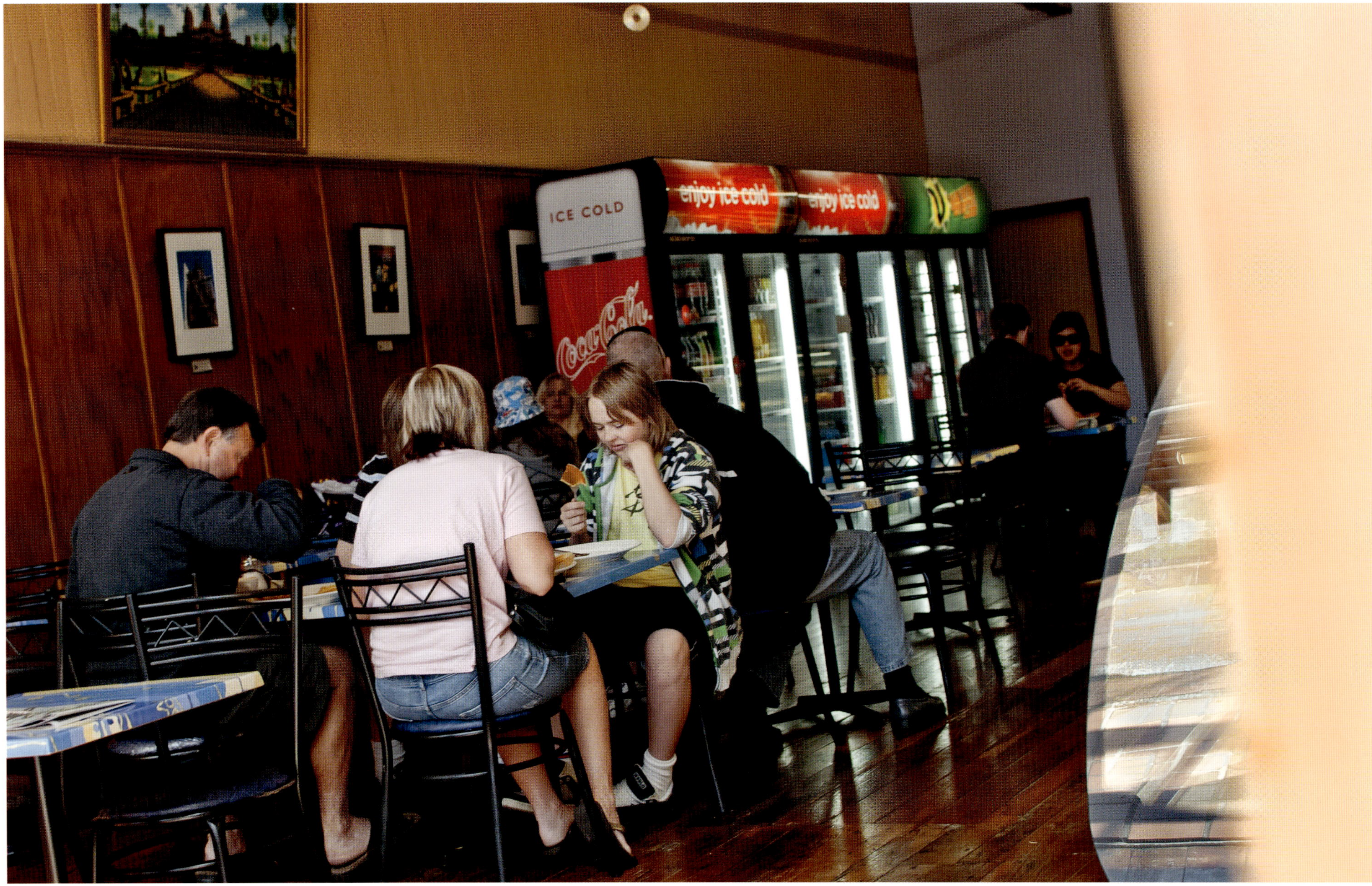
ICE COLD
enjoy ice cold
enjoy ice cold
Coca-Cola

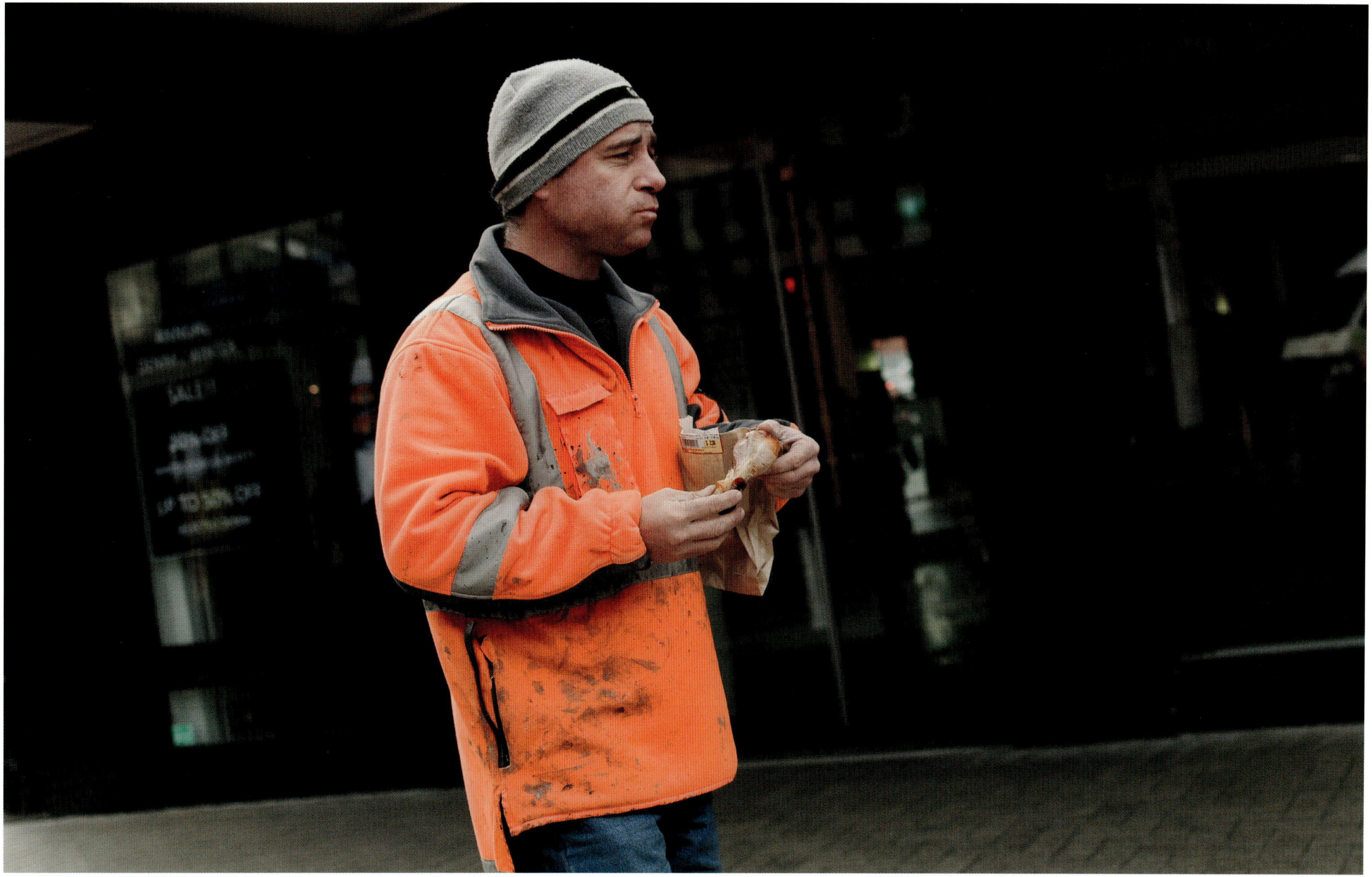

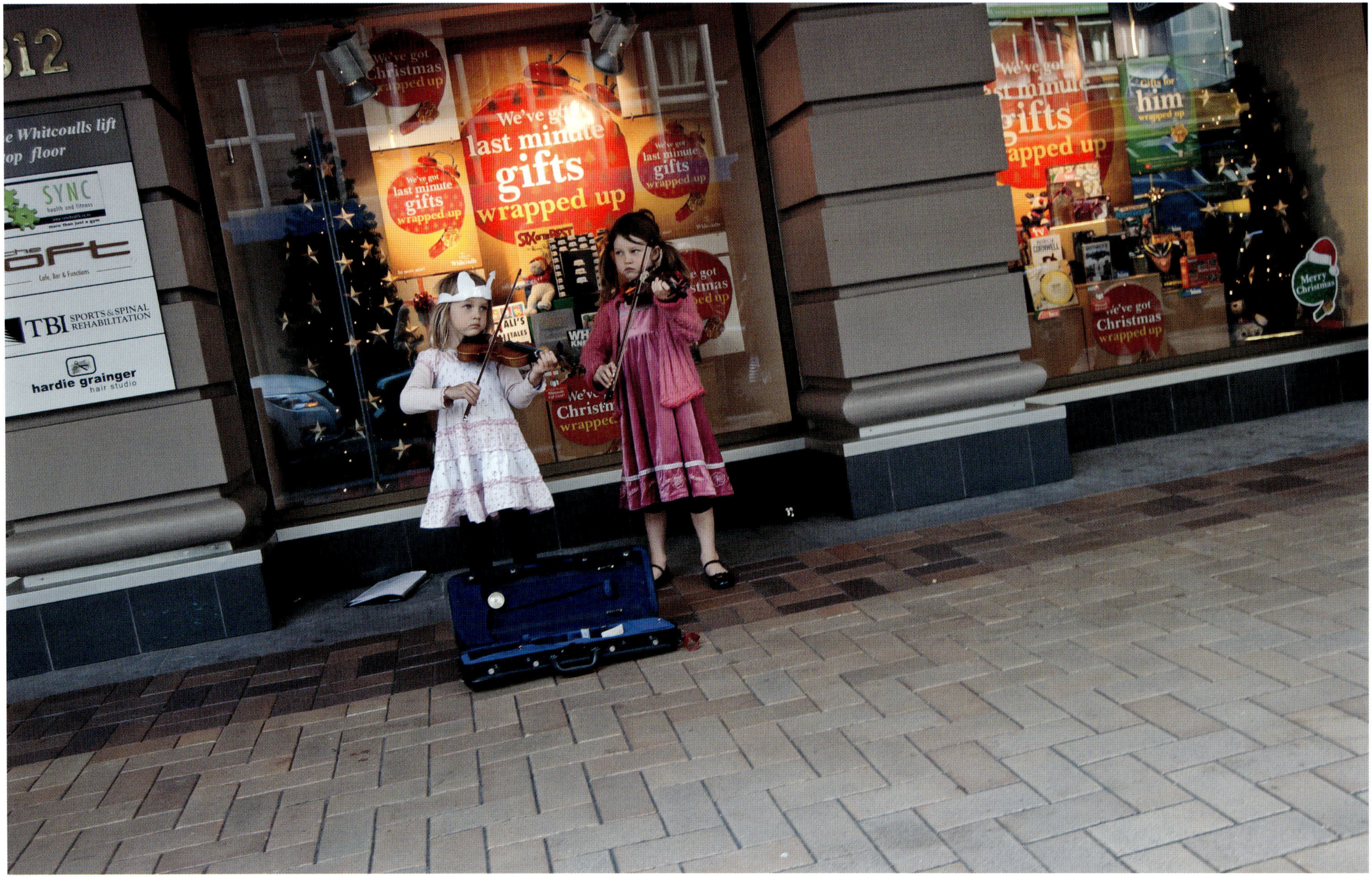

We've got last minute gifts wrapped up
SYNC
TBI SPORTS & SPINAL REHABILITATION
hardie grainger
hair studio
Merry Christmas

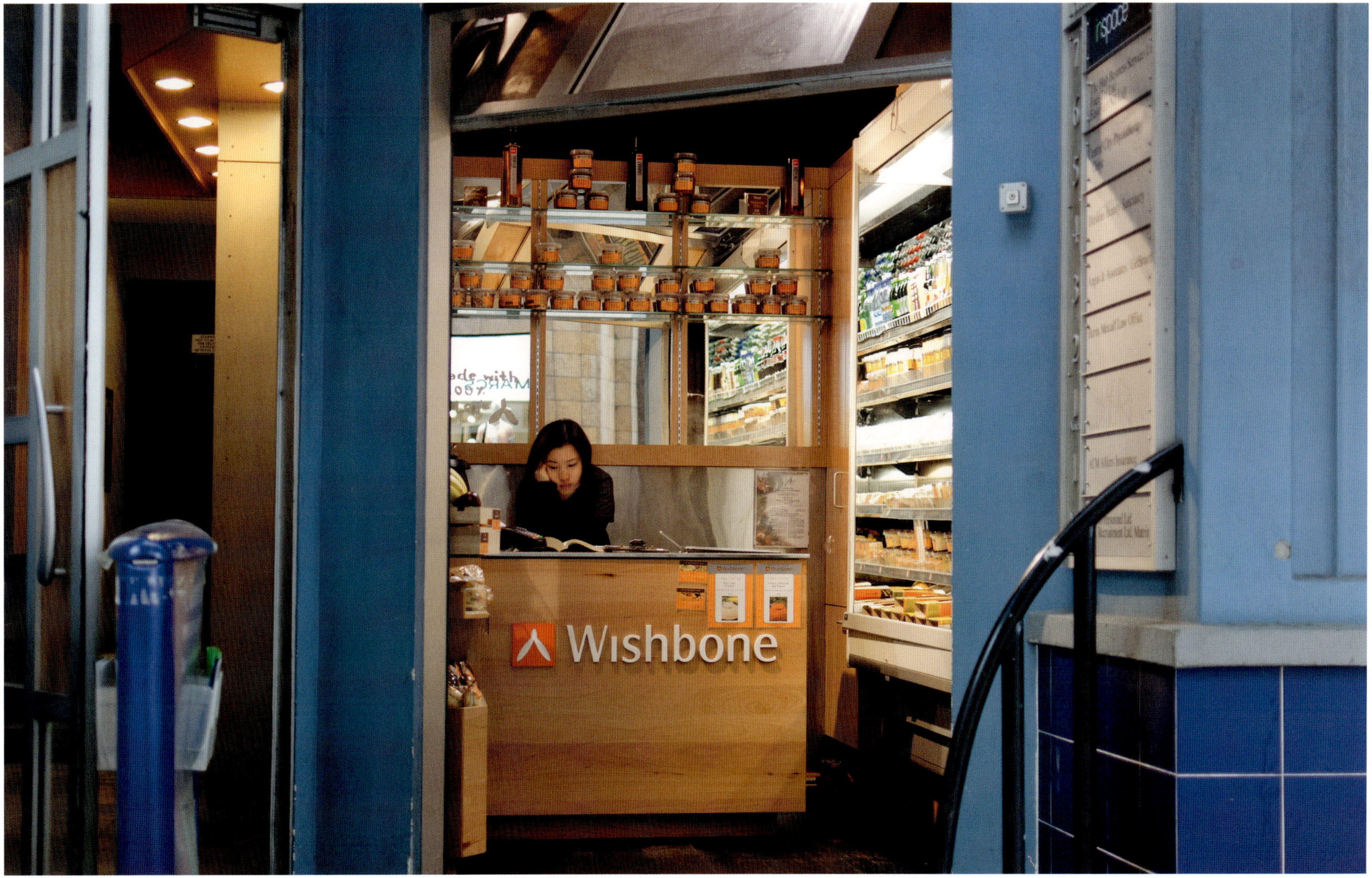
Wishbone

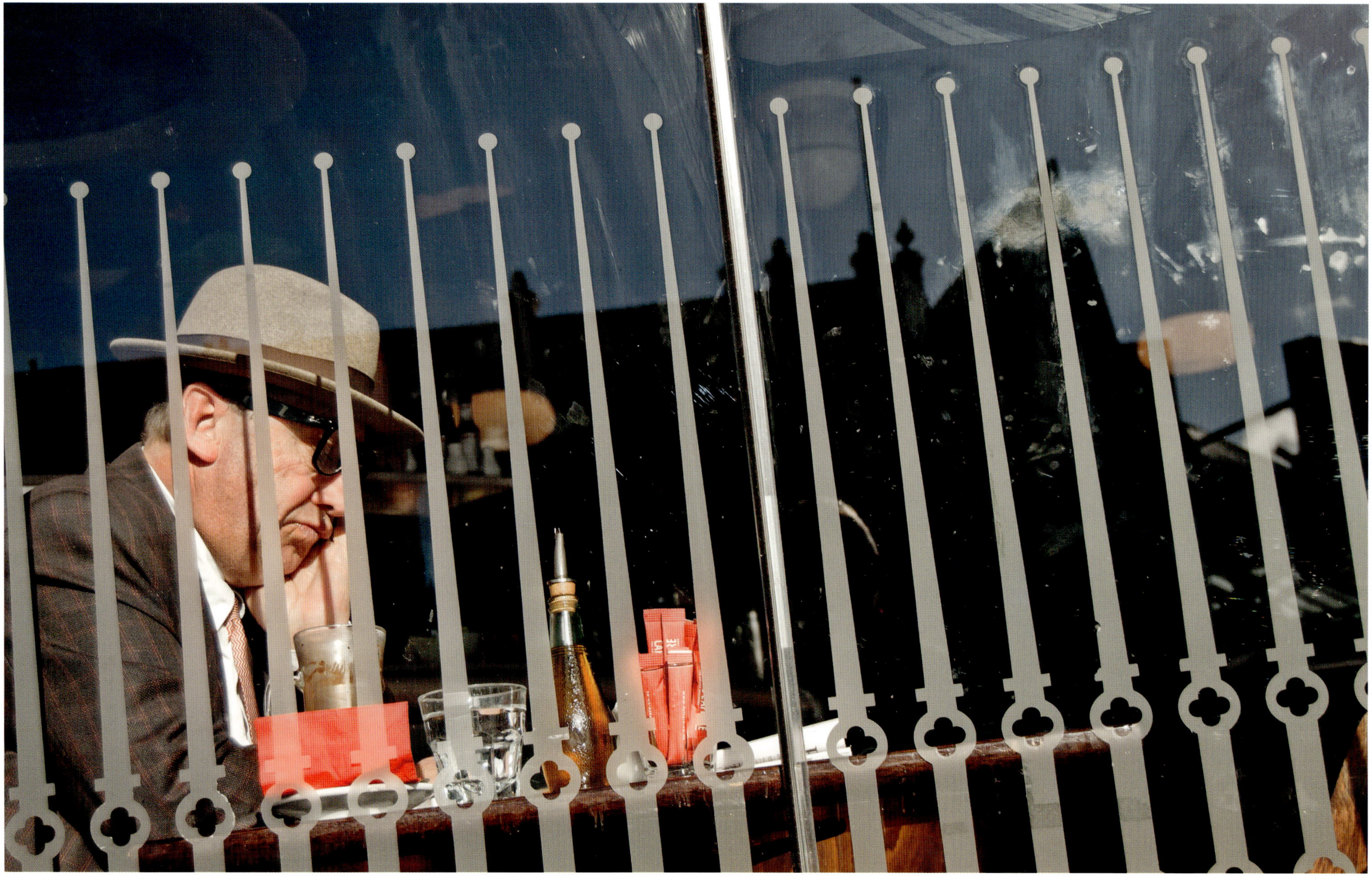

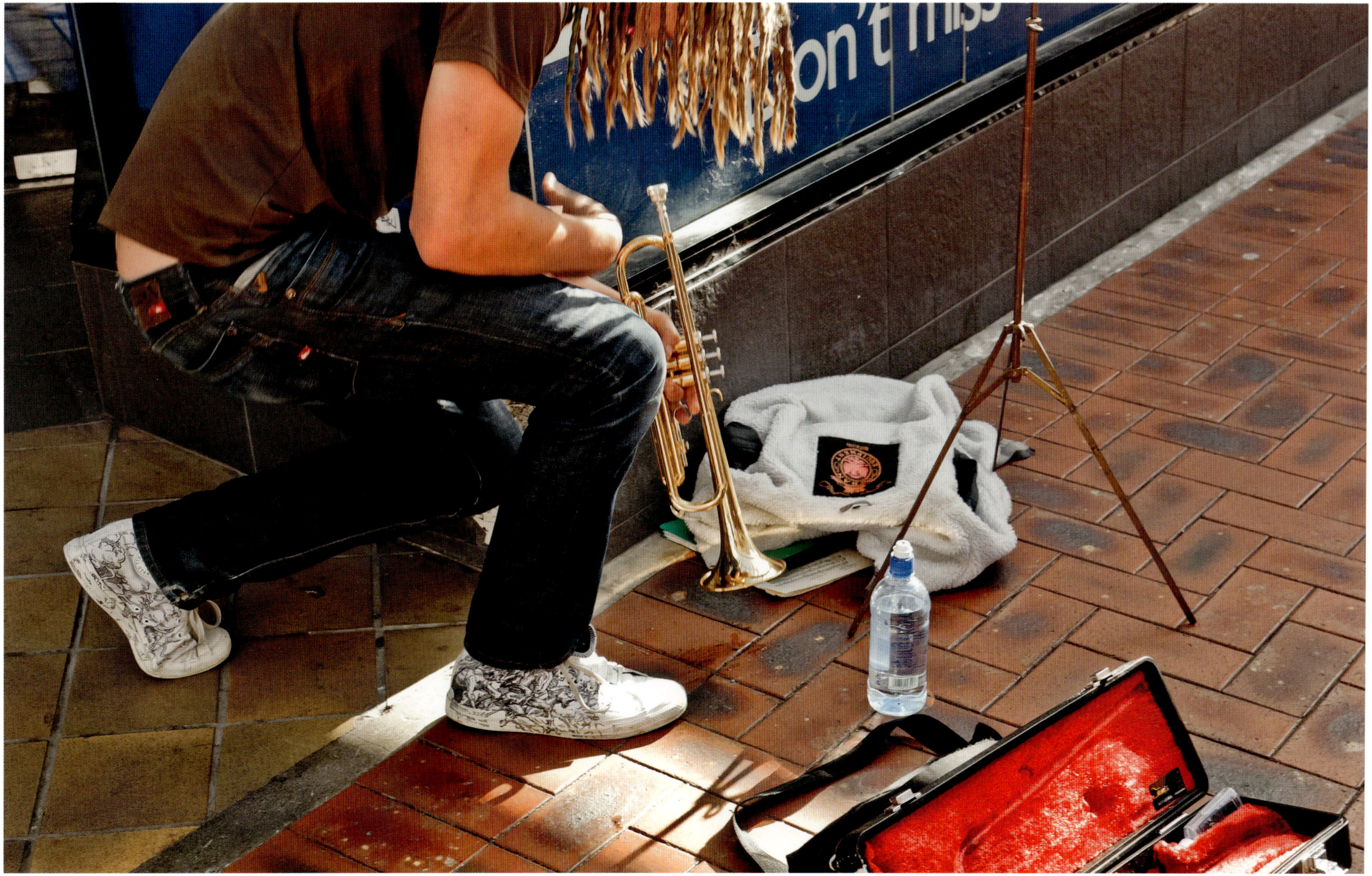

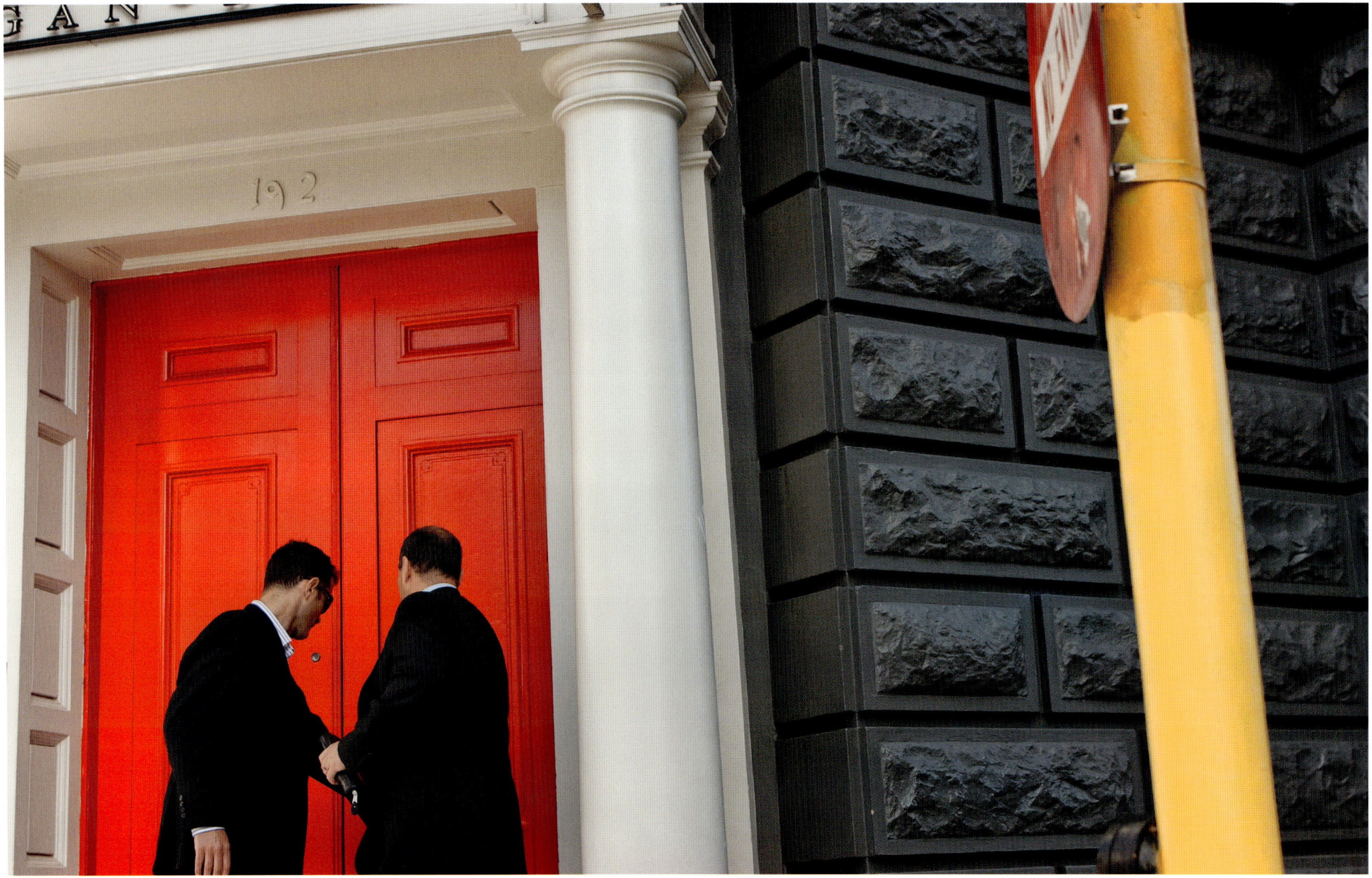
GAN
192

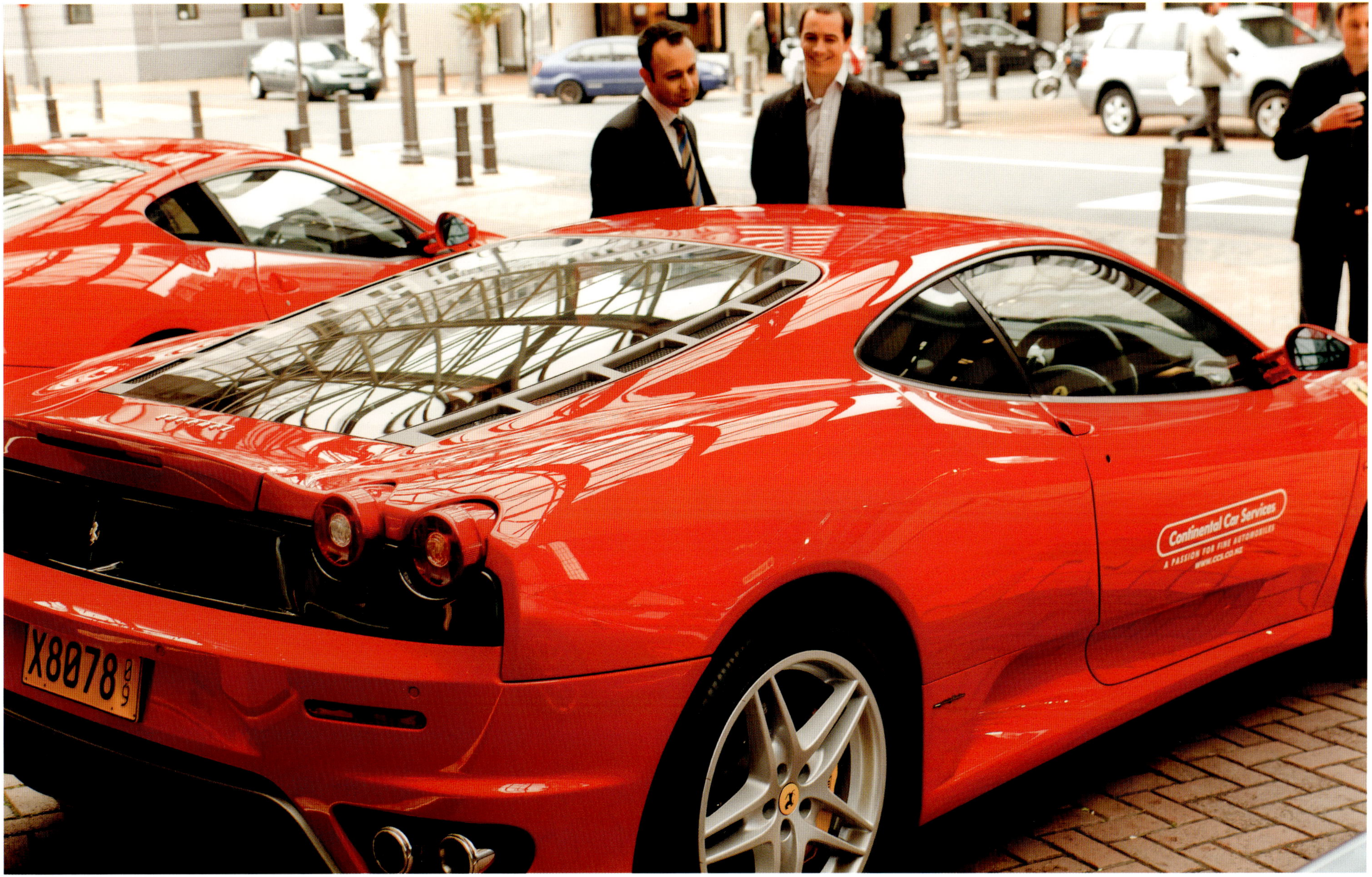
X8078
Continental Car Services
A PASSION FOR FINE AUTOMOBILES

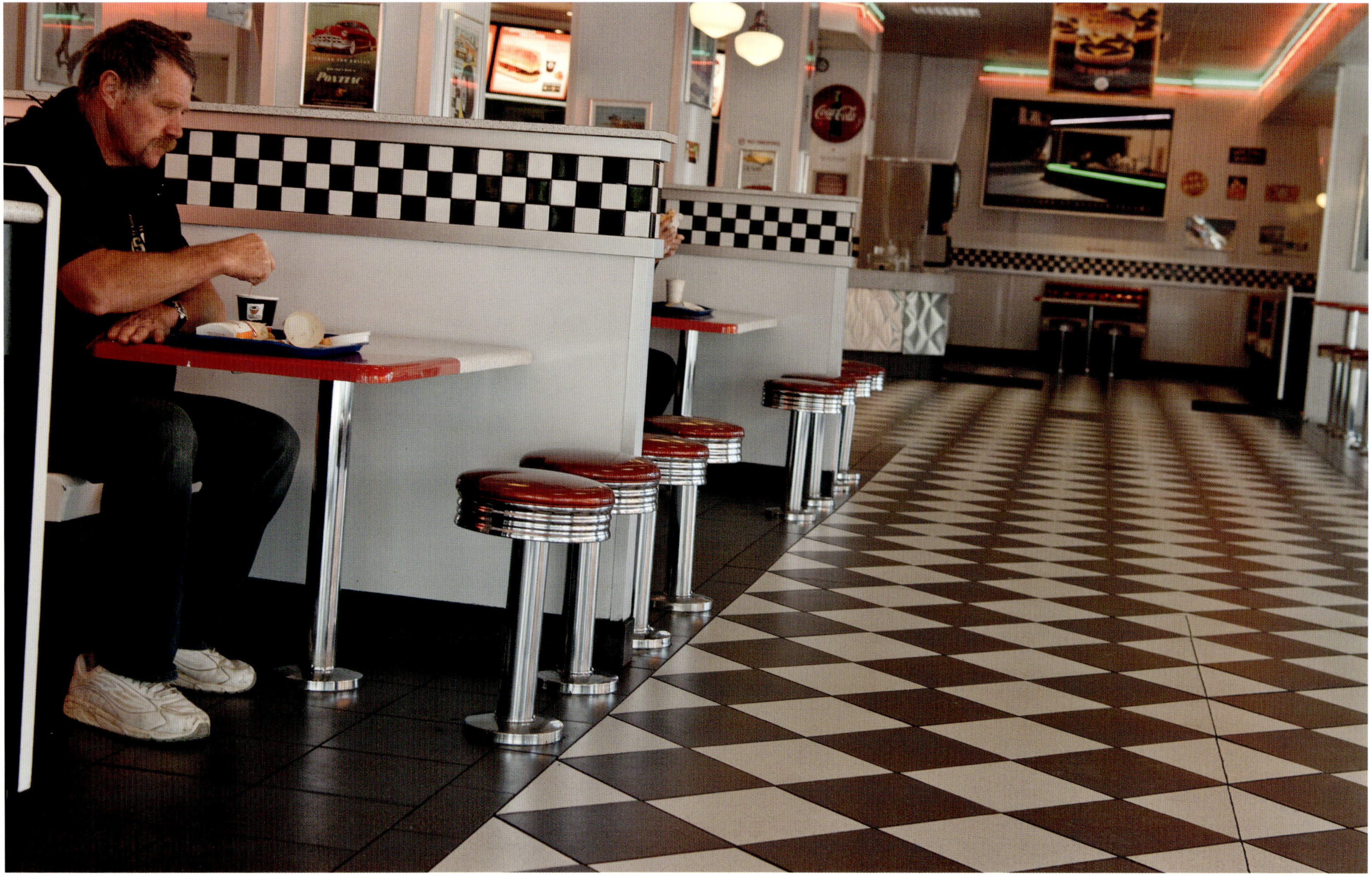
PONTIAC
Coca-Cola

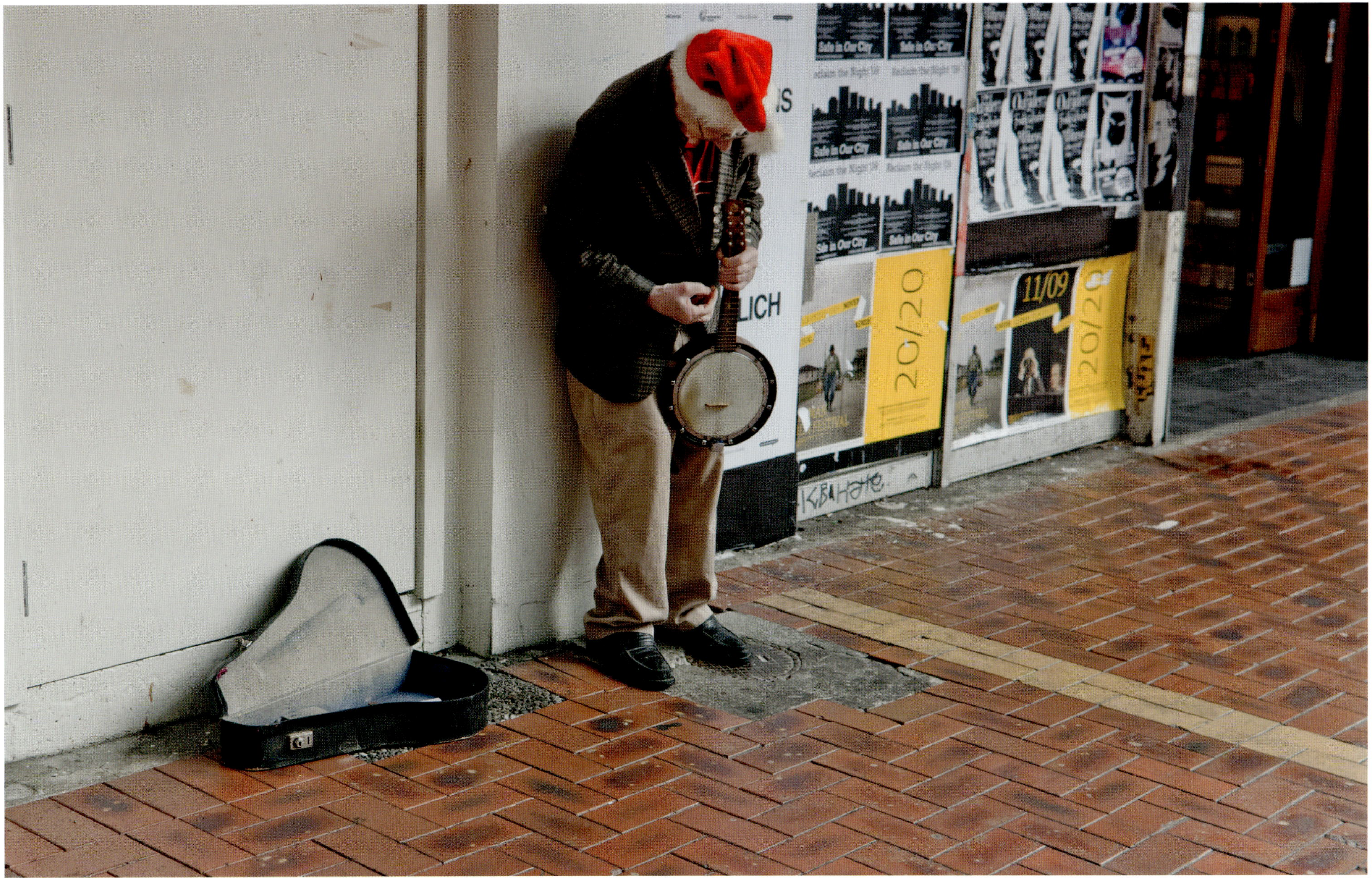
Safe in Our City
Reclaim the Night '09
20/20
11/09

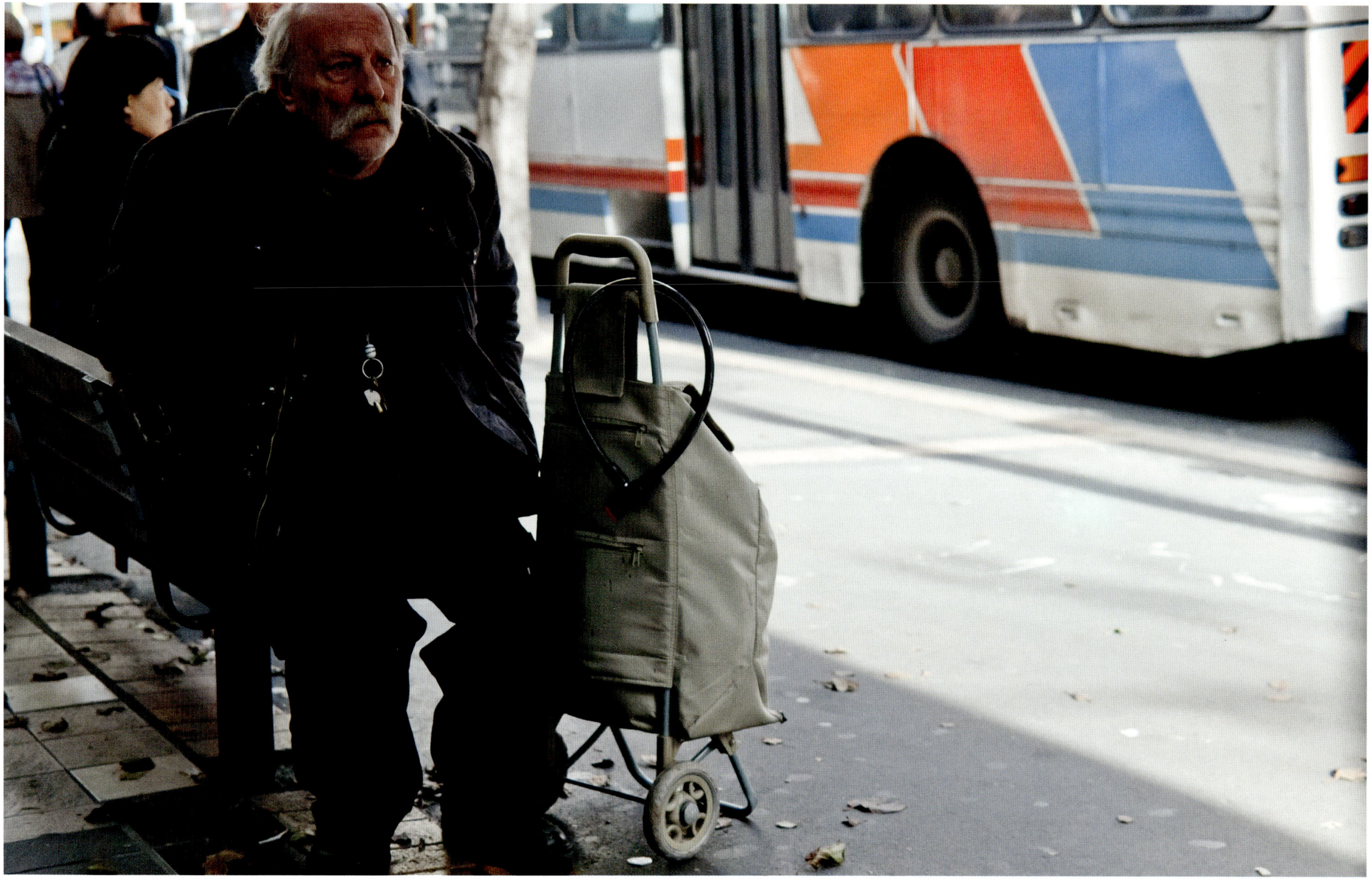

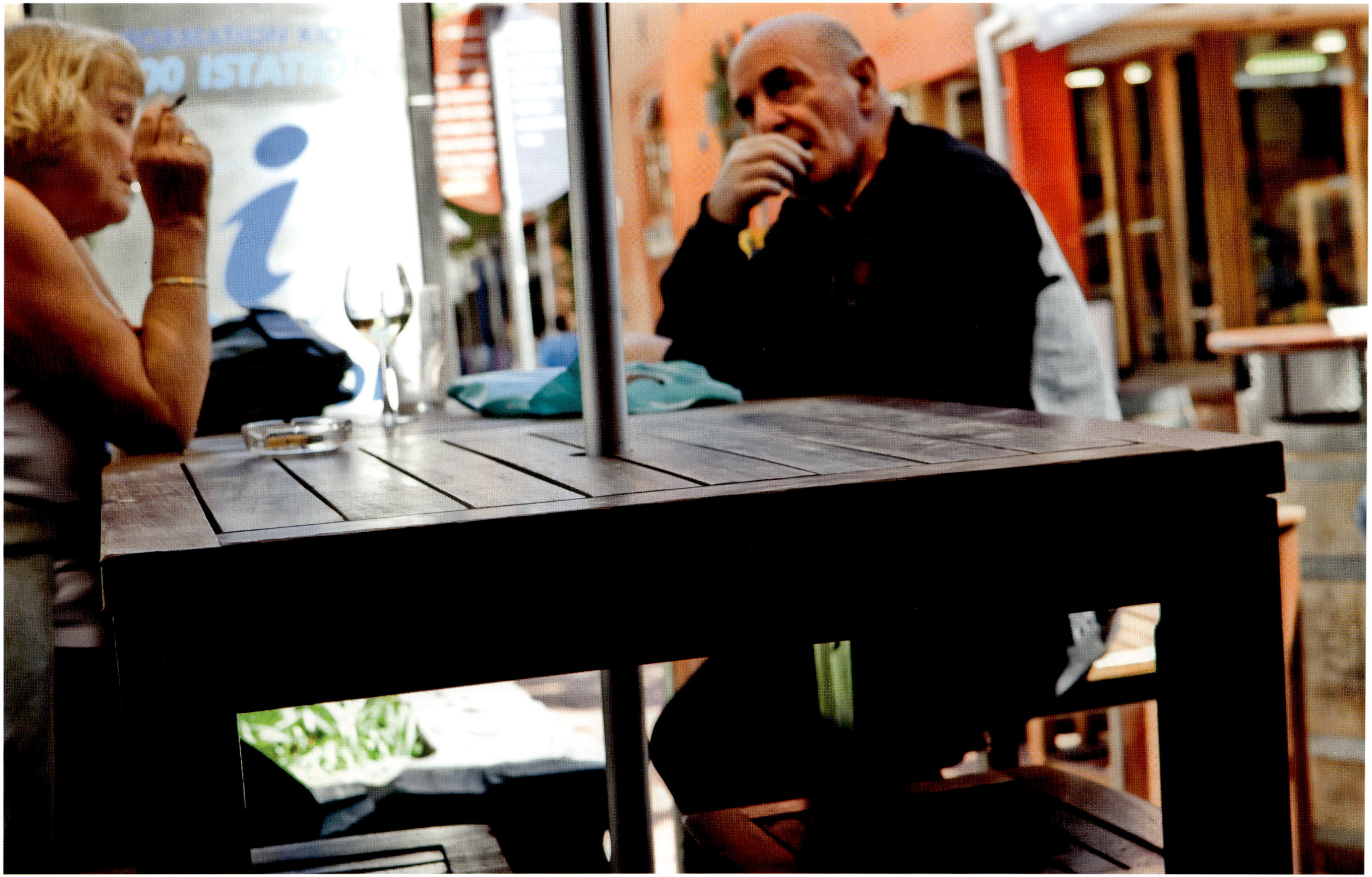

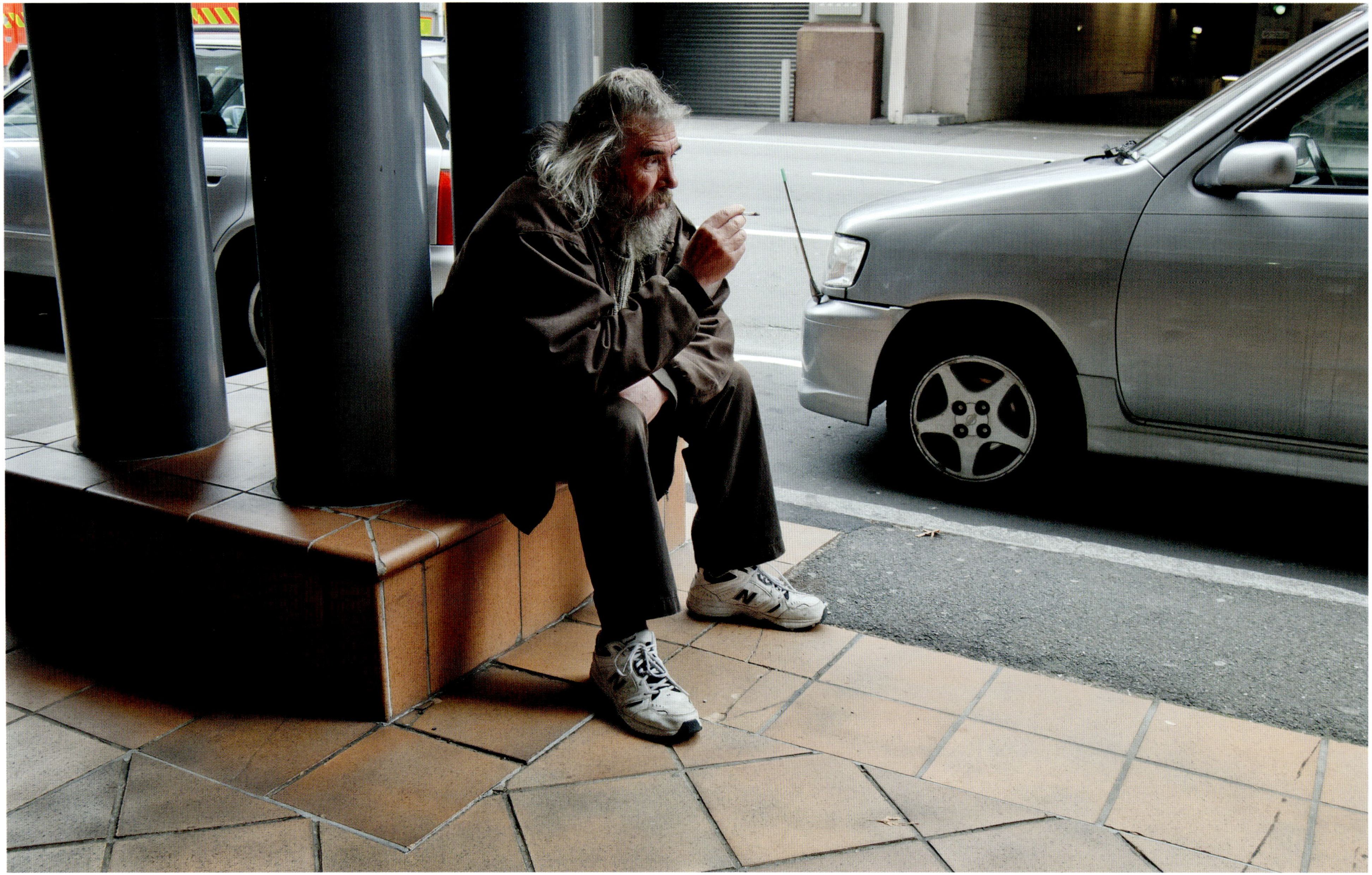

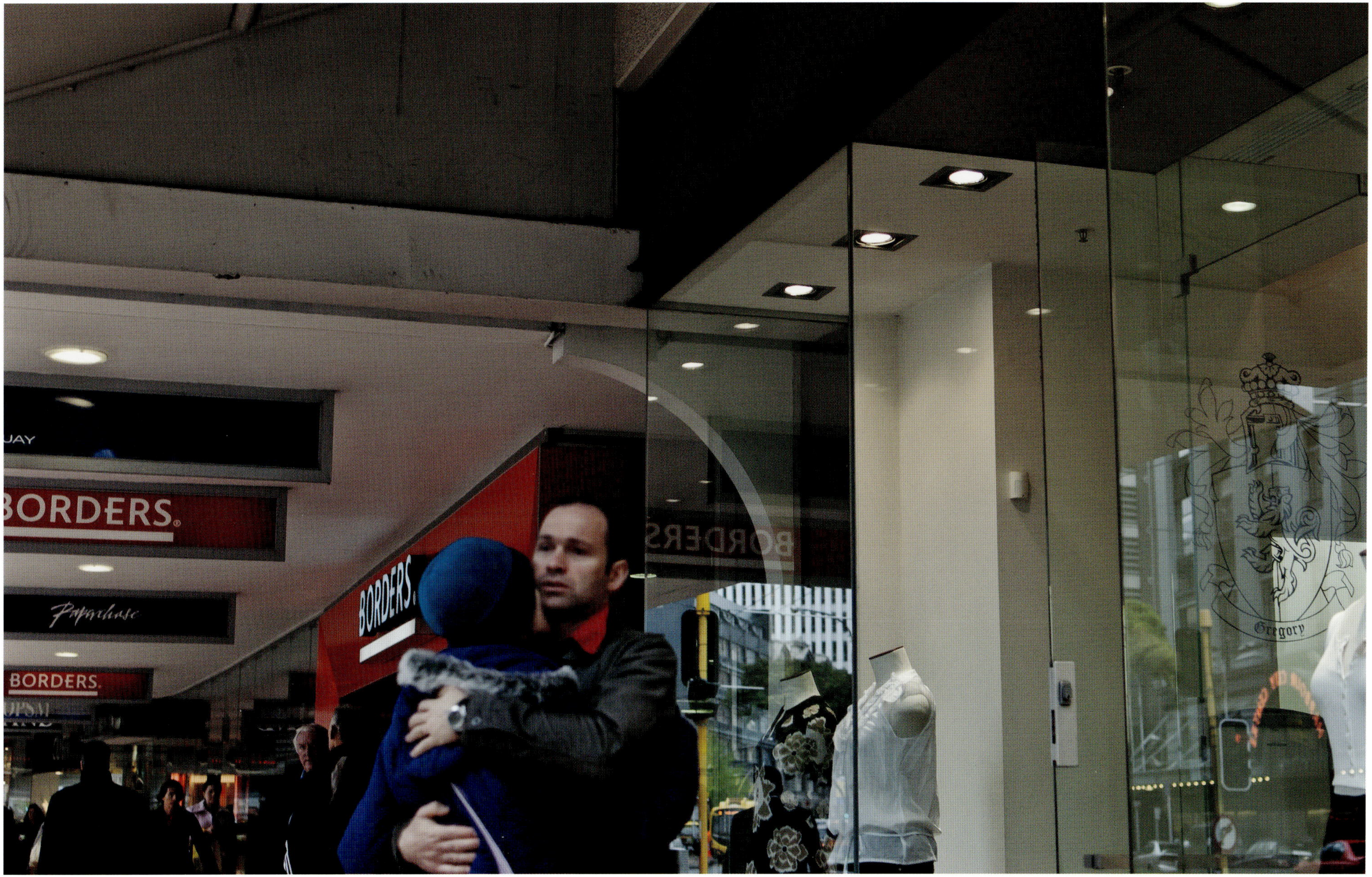
BORDERS.
Paperchase
BORDERS.
BORDERS.
Gregory

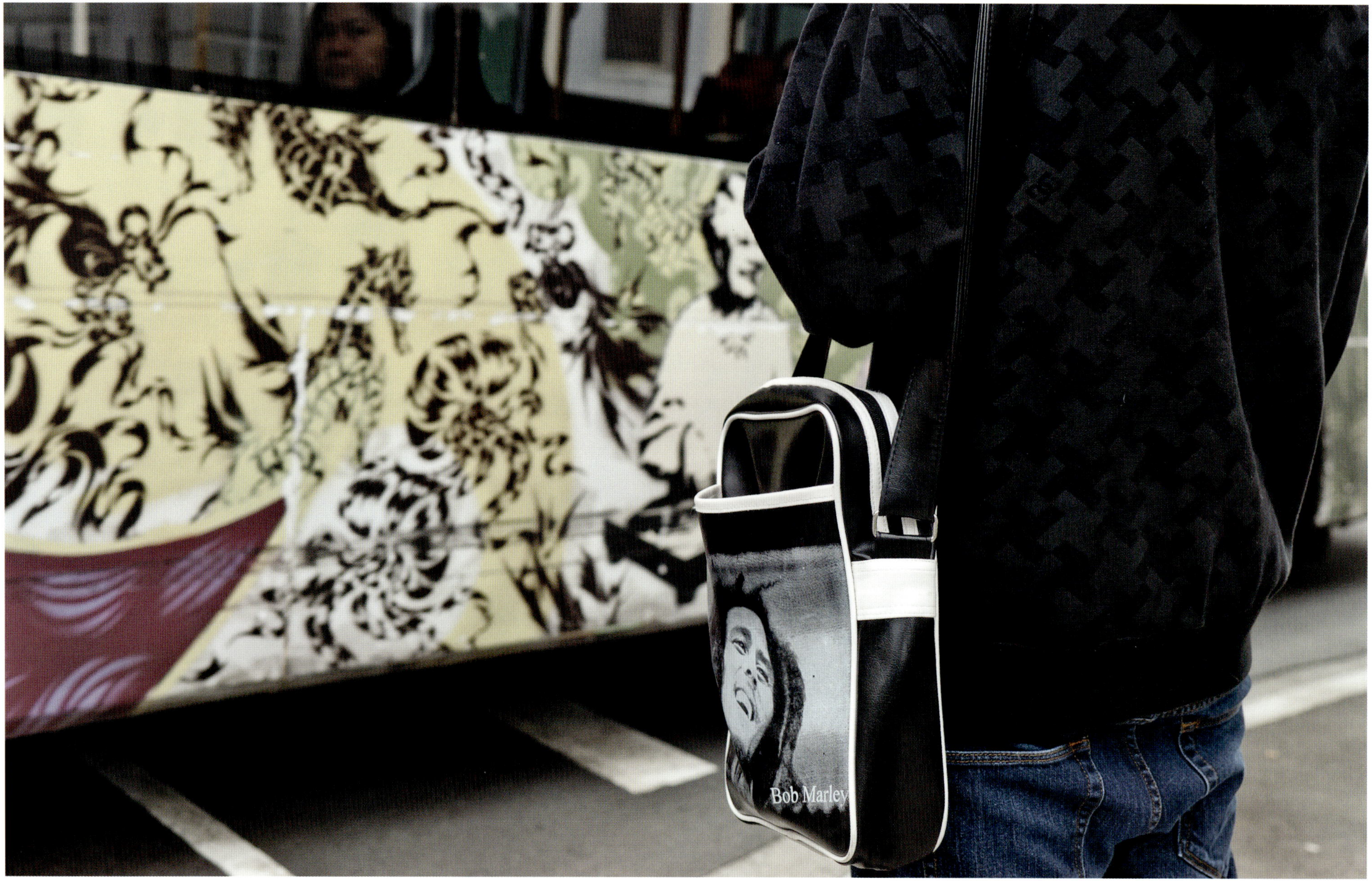
Bob Marley

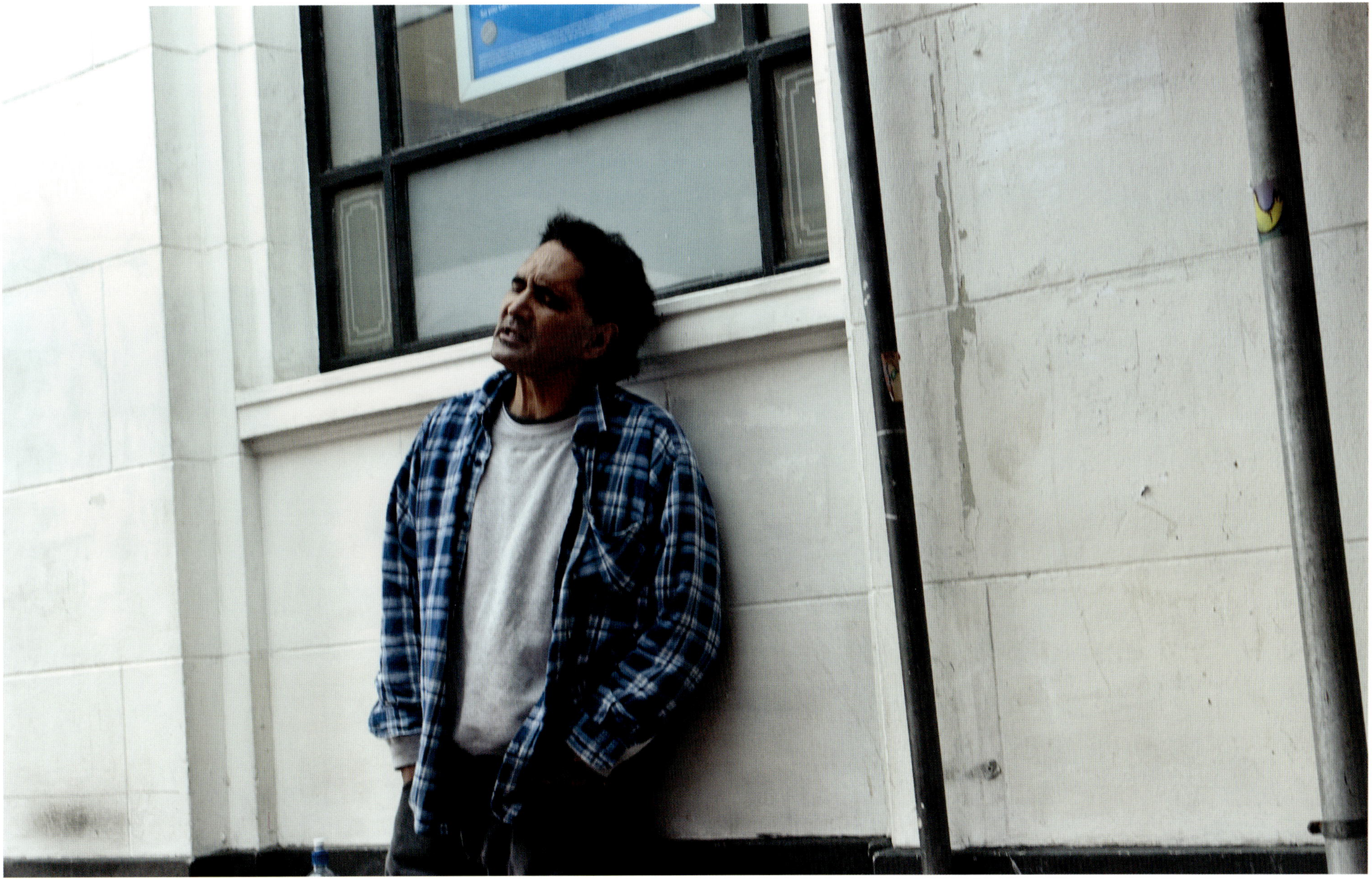

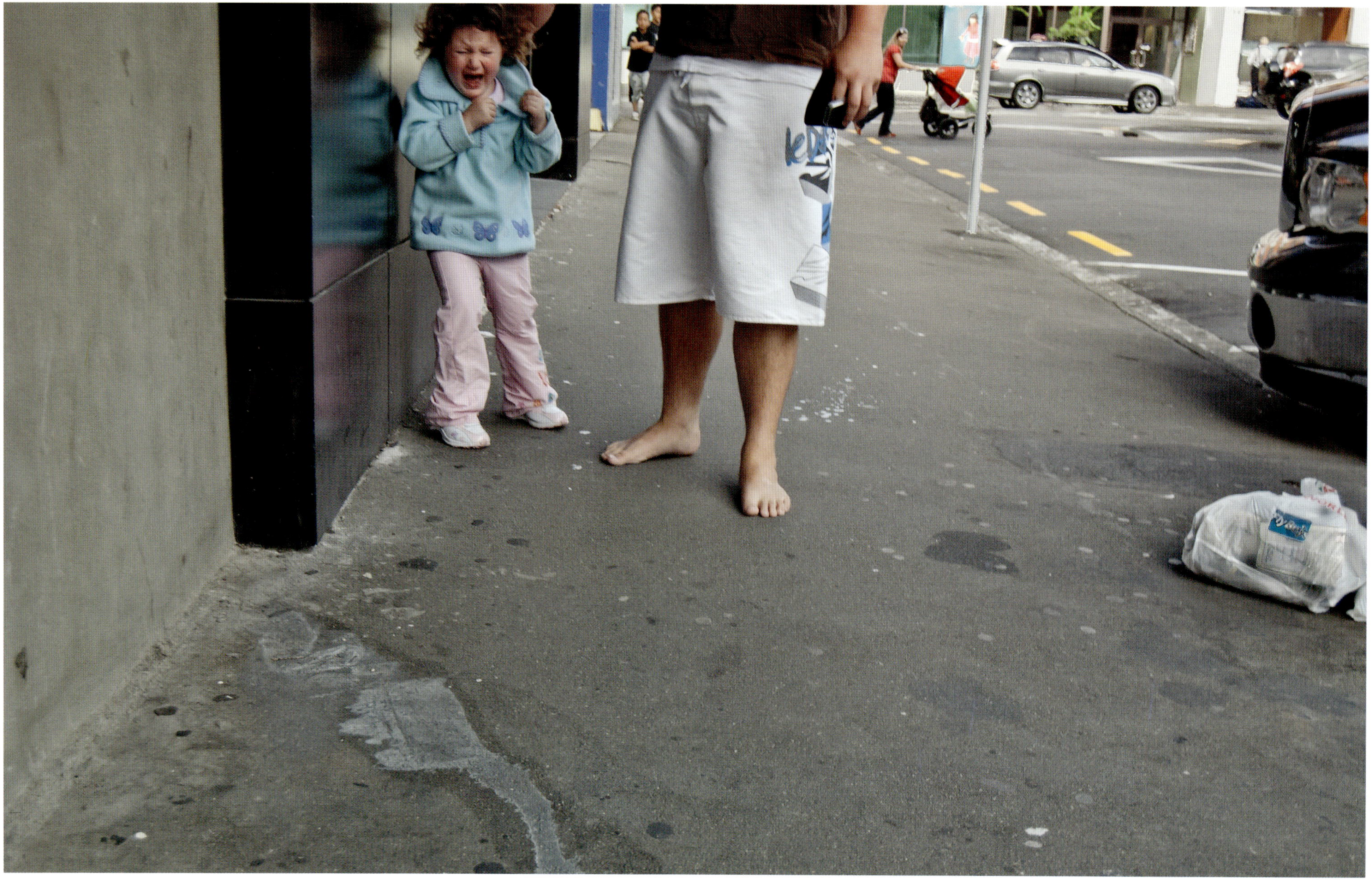

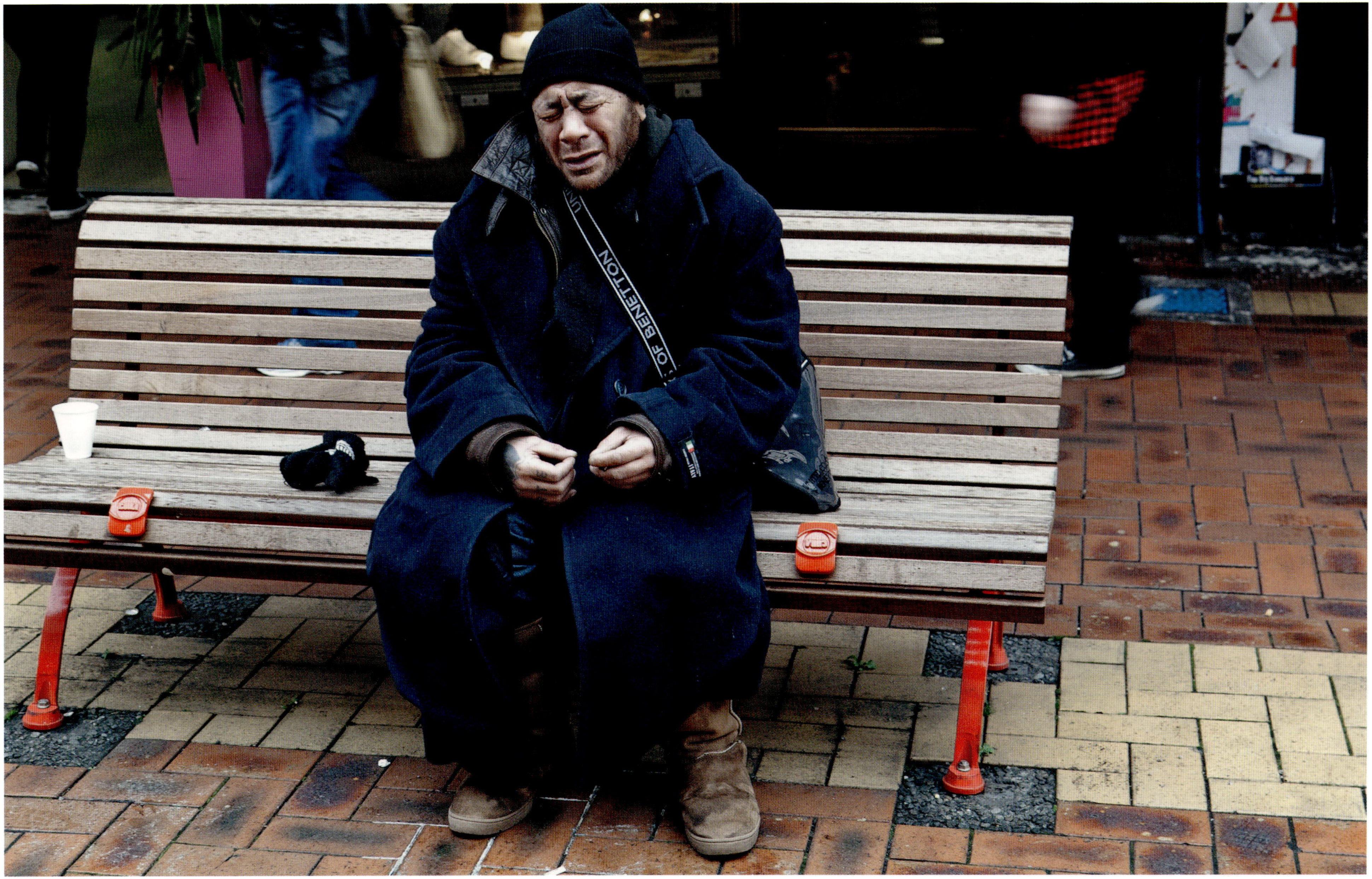
UN
OF BENETTON

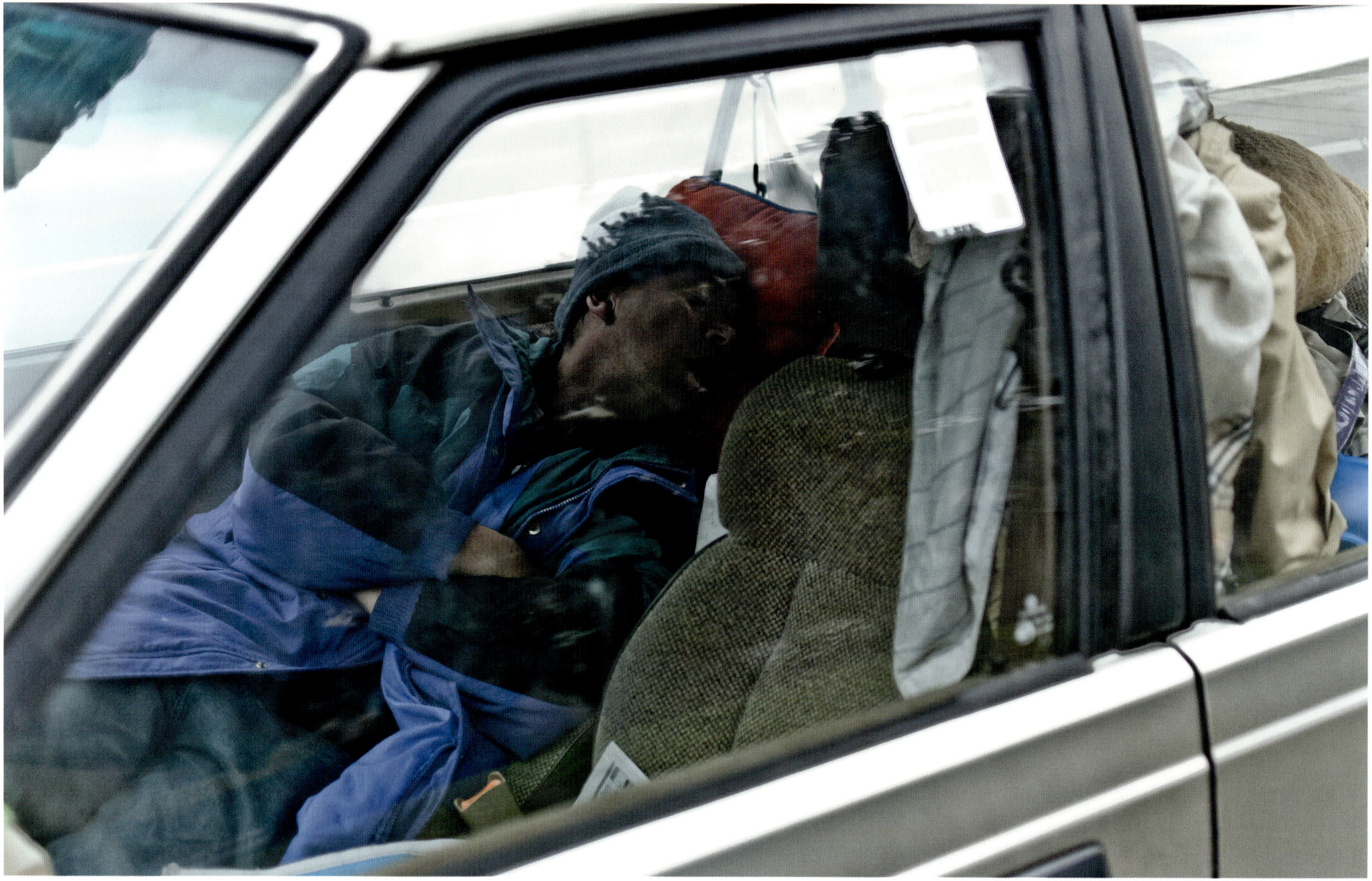

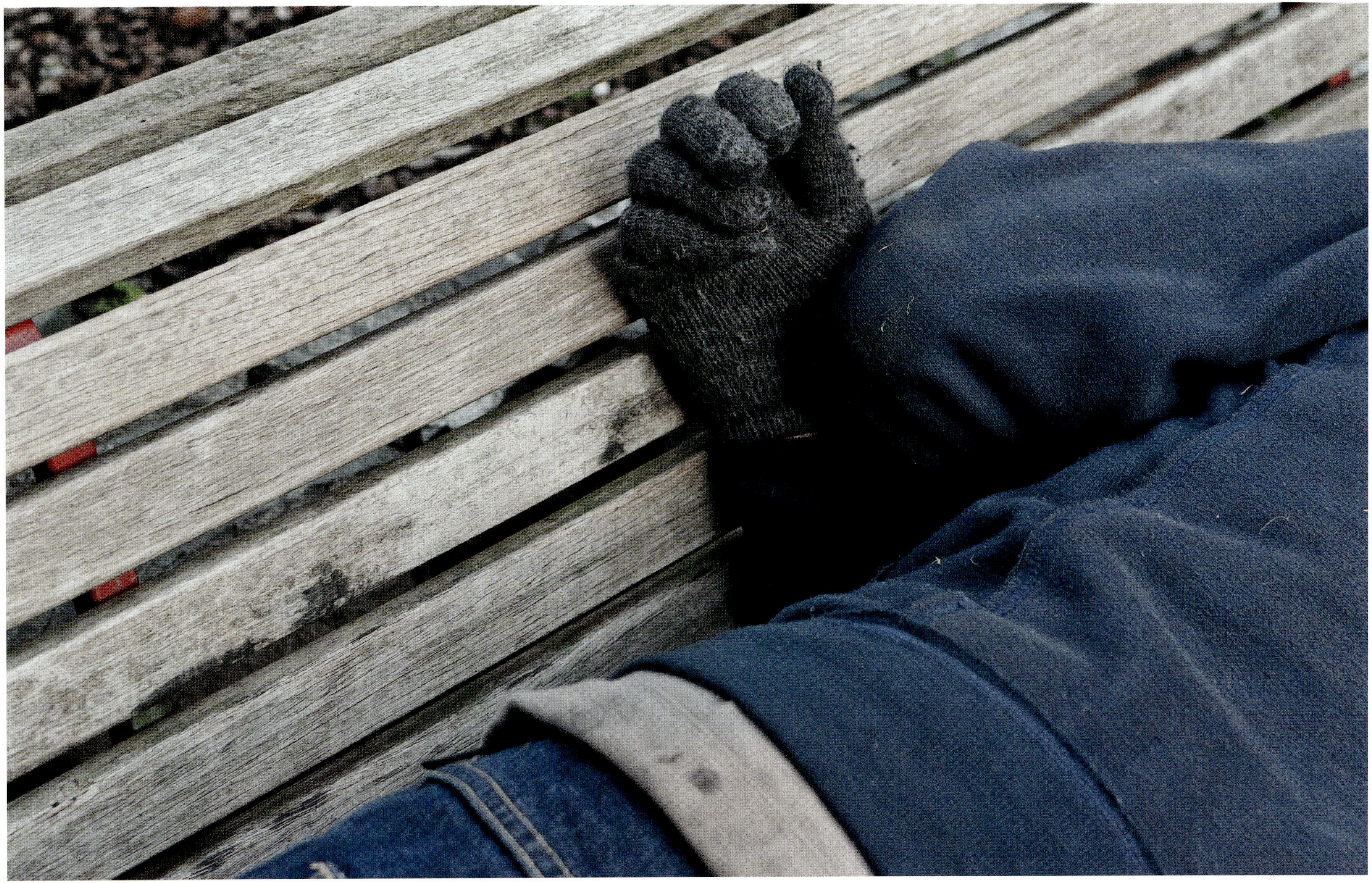

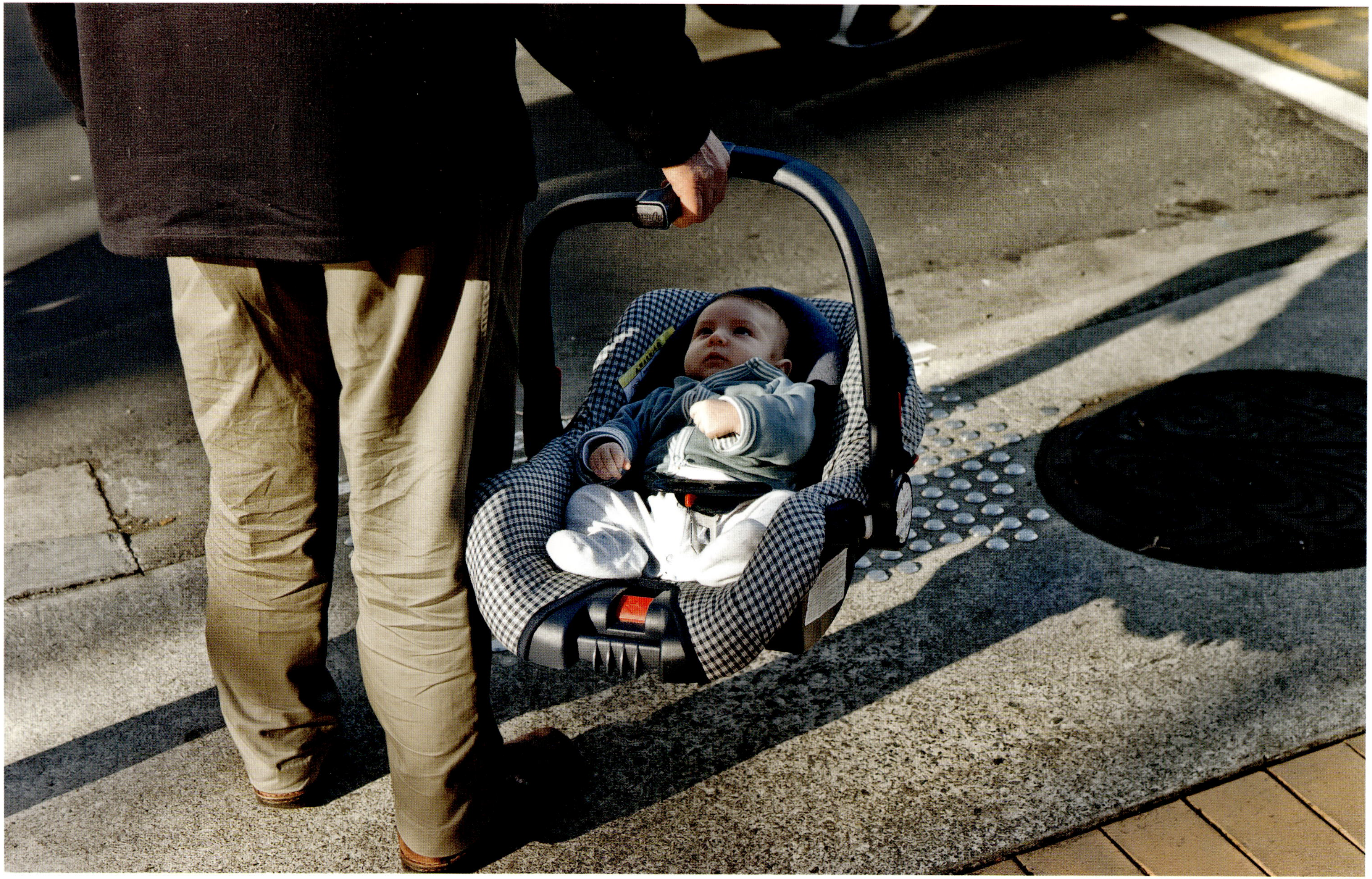

I loved you the moment I saw you

Ian Wedde

Since I moved to Wellington in 1975, almost everything I've written has had a template of one kind or another in this place – the houses I've lived in, the well-worn yet recursively habitual tracks around town, to the post office, through Courtenay Place, Unity Books, the Vietnamese noodle shop on Vivian Street, around Oriental Bay, Moore Wilson's produce, Regional Wines by the Basin Reserve, and so on – routes that are also neural networks or rhizomatic thought-tracks so familiar on a daily basis that I could pretty much walk them at random with my eyes shut. Which, in a sense, I do, as often as not – like anyone else. That partial sightlessness becomes the default state of the habitual urban nomad, the introspective *flâneur*, walking around as if blind to everything but the thoughts or tasks or wishes that occupy the idling mind and are projected there on a screen whose reflexive surface is half turned away from the familiar world outside; or half blind and deaf to anything but the inner narrative that mutters and blinks there in the mind, where language and image are shiftily overriding each other – marking time until I get back to the room I work in, where a familiar disposition of bookshelves, the askance view down across the garden to the neighbour's back yard (which I don't see, because I'm looking at and listening to something mental in between typing) are what fix me in the place of imagination. That this place of imagination is also situated has to be relearned or acknowledged anew from time to time; or I have to be startled into that acknowledgement somehow.

Peter Black's photographs, especially those taken on his own habitual tracks around Wellington, are startling in this way. How often in *I loved you the moment I saw you* we encounter an image that is simultaneously a vivid *aperçu* and a startled, misaligned framing of it – waist-height views that have both noticed people and chopped their heads and feet off, a gesticulating hand inside the refractive light-maze of a café window, the nomad-camera's gaze tilted up to notice a single individual looking down from a row of industrial windows, an anguished face snatched into perception from a passing van. The strategy of these photographs is to deterritorialise their objects at the same time as situating them along the habitual tracks of the nomad-viewer.

If there is indeed a correlation or mirroring between rhizomatic neural networks and the habitual mapping of an environment, then Peter's photographs of Wellington have the effect on me of lighting up that connection. This is not just a matter of recognition – or *re-cognition*, to give the effect a more startling quality – but of intensity, alerting, switch-throwing. Though they reward careful looking, these are not contemplative images. Rather, they are adrenalin shots to my somnolent awareness. They put me back in my place; they wake me up to it.

For thirty years or so there's been a Wellington nexus in the narratives I've been writing, in which that mis-sighted world of imagination has brought together vividly layered memories of place and contrapuntal encounters in the present. Most recently, that narrative has been a screenplay set in and around what Courtenay Place might be like in 2090. This narrative workplace is in effect an archaeological wiring diagram upon which layers of memory are superimposed along with imagined futures – a surface at once refractive and transparent, a shifty and shifting reality of fragments, familiar and uncanny. That view of the future is possible because I already have a layered one to the past; the present is a kind of prism between them.

What is the time of the still image? Like the plate-glass windows in many of Black's photographs of the city, still image-time is a multi-layered laminate that simultaneously contains (and preserves) the moment of the exposure, represents that moment's anachronism, reflects the *situation* and point-of-view of the photographer, implies or partially reveals a story or sequence of events continuing through time, and – because all photographs become retrospective a nano-second after they've been taken – is or metonymises a memory. The individual still image may also be situated in a thematic sequence of images, and so contains within itself the trace or potential of a larger physical time, which is both the cumulative time of the thematic sequence, and the time it takes to turn the pages of a book, click through an on-screen file, or walk the length of a gallery wall.

One of Black's best known portfolios was called *Moving Pictures.* This was and wasn't a pun – it was a riff on 'movies' and 'moving image' (as well, perhaps, as on 'moving' as in emotional) and it was also a deadpan taxonomy of still photographs often taken from the window of a moving car. The images in *I loved you the moment I saw you* have embodied that pun-that-isn't. Each one is a 'frame'. Frames are stitched together in varieties of thematic and narrative sequences. The whole portfolio describes a narrative arc – or circuit perhaps, since it seems to end close to where it began, with the image of a man at a pedestrian crossing with a baby in an infant car seat. And yet the sense of complex time in these new photographs isn't primarily produced by the linear effects of sequential themes or narratives. Such linear time – the time of 'moving images' – is shallow compared to the laminated layers of time in Black's discrete photographs. When these complex laminates are then placed in 'moving' sequences, for example on the turning pages of a book, the effect is of a time-flow slowed by its very thickness; its glassy viscosity; by its thoughtfulness.

This is also, emphatically, digital time. The sharpness, depth-of-field, colour-and-light complexity, translucence, heterogeneity, and multiplicity of many of these images create a *moment* – 'the moment I saw you' – beyond the scope of a more unitary, homogenous analogue time. Though Black's black-and-white analogue photographs were often complex in respect of their wry detail, they don't approach the complexity of his most recent digital colour work. And though this complexity may, at first glance, appear to reside in highly defined and sharply focused layerings of light, colour, and surface, it is fundamentally about the time-frames and time-depths of the photographs.

The visual narrative of a screenplay differs from my more customary writing practice. I notice this difference not so much because of its obvious craft requirements, but because, instead of my lips moving to the silent mutter of drafting words, my eyelids flutter at a mental shuttering of imagined images, and my gaze drifts upward and often to the left, looking and thinking inwardly. When I shift to the registers of language, my gaze drifts downwards under a frown of concentration. These simple mechanics of cognition and visualisation translate into equally simple diagrams of points-of-view. A photograph may mirror or seek to reproduce these, as may the conventions of representation associated with art. Where is the surface of the picture? What are the effects and purposes of perspectival strategies such as *repoussoir*? What is the plane of exchange between the picture and the viewer? What is depth? Where is the narrative junction at which image mutates into language, and vice versa? What is the indexical ratio of inside to outside, image to world? Why are we being manoeuvred into looking *down* (or up) – what are the power relations of the view, its strategies for sublimity? What is the agency of the picture – what kind of society does it network; what kind of viewer socius, and what kind of viewed public? How does (or doesn't) it link these constituencies?

All these familiar questions are reflections or articulations of physical actions and effects. The picture is where effects and affects mesh: the eye-movements and perceptions of the photographer or artist are as much in the picture as the picture's object, whose awareness of being photographed is also an effect – and a subject – in the picture. The picture becomes simultaneously an imaginative construct, the site of emotions, an indexical object, and an archive of mechanical and physiological actions. As well as reproducing the world in some way, and recording (or inviting) emotional responses to it, the picture reproduces the cognitive postures of the artist; and it persuades the viewer to adopt (or react to) those postures. These are what the viewer is responding to, as much as to what the image documents; they also constitute the picture's meaning. And it's the physiological difference between writing images (as in a screenplay) and writing words (as now) that has recently startled me back into acknowledging the *situation* of my perceptions. But, more particularly, it has been looking at the photographs in *I loved you the moment I saw you* that has alerted me to this: to the different ways in which perception is situated, and to the laminated or layered times it takes to take that in – to be moved, to be in love, in '*the moment*'.

For ten years or so, every day began for me with a walk or run with our dog Vincent up around the slopes of Mount Victoria – inevitably the same route or a slight variation on it. Dogs are creatures of habit and I was happy to comply. The dog's and my perceptions and timing fused in some way – a rhythm of movement that was not entirely my own conducted what I saw, heard, and smelled. I looked down at the familiar topography of the city through the filters of senses whose vividness had been reprogrammed briefly away from thoughts of work or the inner screenings of imagination: the colours I saw below me were, for a time, like the chromatic codes of scents, or of information diverted through a warping lens of some kind. Even after Vincent's death, I sometimes feel those filters coming into play as I walk above the abstract social pattern of the city below me; a synaesthesia that seems about to exit the realm of metaphor ('loud colour') and claim a physiological truth. Though Black's colour photographs are complex visual constructs, I feel them warping my sensory habits into a kind of synaesthesia, as though I'm perceiving the familiar world in the company of a commanding but sympathetic cognitive change-agent.

In the 1970s, early in my time in Wellington, I worked as a postie for six years with routes around the southern suburbs and the Cook Strait coast. This was a suburban environment, and different from the city one I now criss-cross daily along familiar paths; but its six-days-a-week repetitions, and the automaton-like perceptions those engendered, where habit might be shocked to attention only by a rushing dog, also shaped the *flâneur*-like habits I have now. I'm used to walking around on a kind of perceptual automatic pilot. When walking the dog, it was a kind of cross-species sensory recalibration that made what was familiar vivid again. When delivering the mail, it was the extreme repetition, letterbox after letterbox, that shut alertness down.

How to put the dog back into the jaded habits of the *flâneur*? It's surely no accident – or at least a happy coincidence – that two of Black's previous books, *white horse black dog* and *Real Fiction*, have photographs of dogs on their covers. These are the human race's most ubiquitous companions; sometimes they are even our 'seeing eyes'; our perceptions and theirs, though mysteriously different, are joined at a cognitive hip. On the cover of *white horse black dog*, the animal has thrust its primary sense organ, its nose, as close as possible to the device that is staring at it, the camera, whose gaze it meets with its own

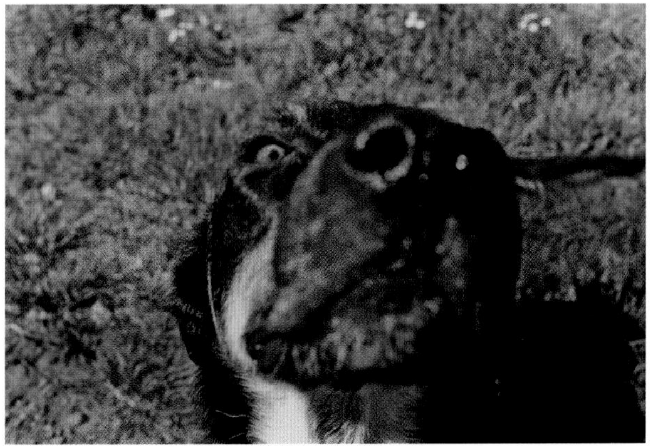

Waihau Bay 1986
(from *Moving Pictures*)

non-visual scrutiny or challenge. The dog's large, moist nostrils resemble eyes; one gleams, while the other seems dilated by the adrenalin of perception. Set back, like a secondary organ, is a small, demented eye, glaring with a kind of desperate subaltern effort; the nose has it. What this image, long one of the favourites in Black's oeuvre, seems to be proposing is a radical rewiring or even dehierarchicalising of our responses – an alternative perceptual set, quite seductive and pleasant, congenial rather than disturbing.

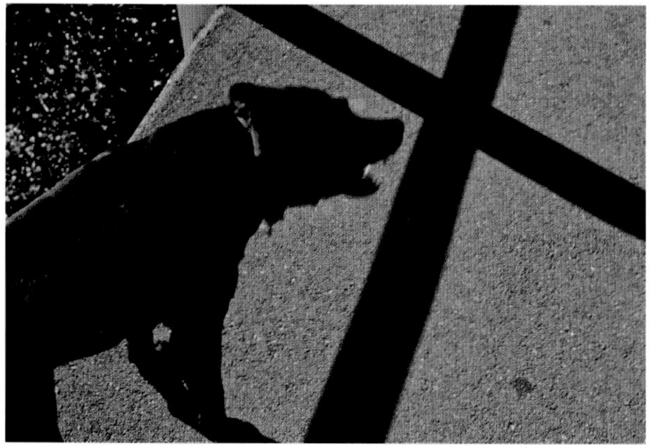

Black Dog and Cross 1984
(from *Real Ficton*)

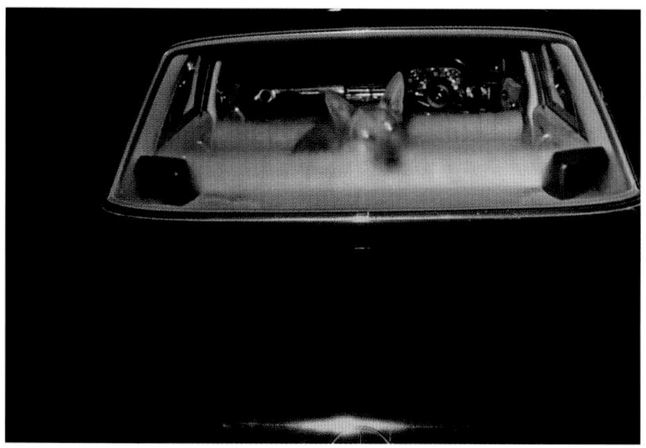

Dog and Mercedes Benz 1978
(from *Fifty Photographs*)

On the cover of *Real Fiction* another dog, more aggressive than curious this time, appears as a cross between itself and its shadow, its bark seeming to appear as a single blazing, tooth-like flash of light within its open jaws. The plane of the photograph is deeply ambiguous: what must be the ground on which the dog is standing seems to tilt almost vertically, the dog (or its shadow) seems not so much to be standing on this ground as projected against it; and what seems to be the object of the animal's aggression, the shadow of a cruciform structure, presents the illusion of occupying the same two-dimensional plane as the dog, as if we were watching a shadow-puppet screen with only minimal distinctions between silhouette and depth. What the image seems to be proposing is a deranged view of the world, in which reprogrammed perspectives, planes, shadows and solids, are wrenching our cognitive faculties into new modes of reception. Our bewilderment or disorientation might resemble the dog's; like it, disturbed and angry, we end up barking at shadows. Or like an earlier dog, the Australian Kelpie looking out the rear window of a car at night in 'Dog and Mercedes Benz' from the 1982 portfolio *Fifty Photographs*, all our senses seem to have been trapped and reprogrammed as if by the action of photography: the dog's eyes blinded, its muzzle blurring into foggy out-of-focus, its ear-pricked hearing blocked by two car stereo speakers.

The photographs in *I loved you the moment I saw you* have put the dog back in the over-habituated perceptions of the urban nomad. They bring about a derangement of senses, sometimes amiable and pleasant, sometimes making our hackles rise in fear and anger. It's not clear whether this effect is what Black has intended should happen to us; whether it's what has happened to him; or whether (as I prefer to think) the photograph is the agent that has linked – networked – these two options in a fluid transactional space in which subject, object, and spectator move in and out of each other.

This portfolio by Black is not his first departure from the black and white works for which he's known and esteemed – *Made in New Zealand* (1984), *Outskirts* (2008) and the ongoing investigations of *New Colour* (2009) are strikingly coherent in their own right. But *I loved you* may be the substantial body of work that establishes Black's carefully developed mastery of the complexity and richness of digital colour, and of the printing technologies that have grown with the medium.

The title of this new portfolio of colour photographs contains a number of clues to how he looked at what he photographed, and how we might look at the photographs he took. The title of the portfolio is an almost-correct quote of the well-known line of the George Harrison song 'For You Blue', on the B side of the Beatles' 'The Long and Winding Road' and the eleventh track on their final album *Let It Be*. But Harrison wrote 'I loved you *from* the moment I saw you', which suggests a whole different focus from Black's.

Nothing is as accidental as it may first seem in a photograph by Black; nor, I believe, is his slight adjustment to the Harrison lyric. To say you loved someone or something *from* the moment you saw them puts that moment in the past and the viewer in a present that is joined to the past by continuous love over linear time. But this sentimental trajectory snaps tight in Black's rewrite, and in his photographs. Each photograph is distinctly in its *now* – the attention, the emotion, the object, the photographer, utterly and sometimes painfully present, however complex the layerings of time may be in that present. The attention of each photograph is minutely observant of details, though these are not the products of a Cartier-Bresson type *instantané* or 'decisive moment': the detail of Black's photographs is dense and thoughtful, and coheres into themes over the course of the portfolio. What he makes into a photograph seems to consist as much of his own intensely compacted thought and observation as of an intuitively noticed event. The photograph's *mass*, if you like, its density of thought, detail, emotion and thematic, slows it down, giving the present in which Black loves what he sees an unmistakable gravity.

Not that these images lack humour. They are full of it, but it's wry and disenchanted; the *love*, as we have already noticed in Black's adjustment to the Harrison lyric, is unsentimental; and the grief and sometimes anger that we sense around images of suffering or deprivation are never patronising. Even the satirical bite that marks some images of privilege or self-satisfaction is without rancour. This emotional maturity or equanimity is won against the sometimes hectic grain of the images – the complexity of their detail, their fervent colour, their narrative ambiguity and richness, their tricky surfaces. This is a paradox of sorts – emotional coherence persisting through a compounding turbulence of successive, vividly present moments.

A list of what emerges as paradoxical from Black's moments of seeing and loving will include the following: the surreal absurdity of the real; the patterned choreography of random chaos; the surface of depth – and, reflectively, the depth of surface; the incoherence of informative signage – and, conversely, the strange coherence of meaninglessly aggregated signs; the humour of gloom; the cheerlessness of a colourful world; the dignity of sad people; the clownishness of serious people.

Above all, perhaps, a sense of paradox surrounds the pervasive loneliness in these images. Among the many themes that can be found in this portfolio, loneliness may be the most prevalent. Yet it nearly always manifests itself in a vividly social environment, without the conventional props of desolation or alienation, in bustling streets, busy eateries, or places densely layered with social commodities – fashion-ware, jewellery, entertainment. What happens in these situations is a kind of ransom switch: the lonely individual appears self-sufficient and without need of the supports on offer; and the congenial environment takes on a melancholy, almost beseeching appearance, as if it's trying too hard to maintain a cheerful, gregarious expression. It's an expression we soon see through, not least when turning the pages of *I loved you the moment I saw you*.

In the first photograph of *I loved you the moment I saw you*, a man, perhaps a grandfather by his cautious stoop and wrinkled hand, is just putting down or is about to pick up a baby in a portable infant car-seat. The baby's eyes are barely open, as if it's just at that very moment waking up and seeing the grandfather. They are at a pedestrian crossing – a potentially dangerous place, though there are no passing cars in view, and the man's gesture seems appropriately careful and solicitous. In the final, eighty-second image of the portfolio, the man has picked the infant car seat up, a car is rushing past close to them, and the baby's eyes are fully open, looking up at the grandfather.

Time has passed between these two images – the time of eighty perceptions. In the blink of an eye, in the time it has taken for the baby to wake up and see (love) its grandfather, the time it has taken for him to pick the baby up and for a car to speed past them, we have criss-crossed the entire city along routes marked out by unique, random perceptions and by subtly choreographed threads and themes. The slicing hand gesture of a young woman in a graduation-day tableau is followed by the outstretched hand signal of a little girl in a fluffy pink coat that might almost be parodying academic dress, and this by the hand-to face gesture of a well-dressed man talking on a cell-phone at a café, this by the sad image of a man clutching his face in a passing van. The red interior of a busker's trumpet case segues into the red door of the up-market Logan Brown restaurant about to be entered by two men in suits, this to the shining red of an expensive sports car being admired by two men, this to the red-highlighted interior of a Burger King restaurant where a single man is stirring his coffee, and this to the red Santa-hat of another busker preparing to play his banjo. Across the organised grain of such curated or narrativised images drift other themes and storylines, some to do with content, others with perception – privilege and underprivilege, the body-languages of power and abjection, street people, brown paper bag drinkers, the strut and pomp of businessmen in suits, the affectionate gestures of friends and lovers, the isolation of individuals; the shattered compositions of reflections, the emotional focus-pulls of perspective, planar switches between lateral and frontal. The apparent randomness of this nomadic wander through the streets of the city coheres over and over again into narrative meaning, sometimes by theme, sometimes by colour, sometimes by cohesive sequences of light and refraction, often by all of these at once.

Of course this is the product of the photographer's homogenising decisions about order and sequence, as also of his editing decisions – we know or intuit that much has been left out. But the rigour of this organising and composing discipline doesn't contradict the larger heterogeneous truth of *I loved you the moment I saw you* – that the moment of love, that perceptual blink of an eye, contains a multiplicity of instances, a compacted shuttering of times, a derangement of senses and perceptions, a fluid network of narratives: a world at once anarchic and disordered, and full of meaning; or perhaps a world that is disordered and *therefore* full of meaning.

Ian Wedde was born in 1946. He is a poet, novelist, critic, and curator. His essays have been collected in *How to be Nowhere: Essays and Texts 1971–1994* (VUP 1995) and *Making Ends Meet: Essays and Talks 1992–2004* (VUP 2005). From 1994 to 2004 he was head of art and visual culture at the Museum of New Zealand Te Papa Tongarewa. In 2009, Auckland University Press with RGAP (UK) published his monograph *Bill Culbert: Making Light Work*. He has written about Peter Black's photographs previously in *Moving Pictures* (1990) and *At Home in the Dark* (2003).

Locations

For some years Peter Black has been walking around Wellington with his camera and making what is in effect a portrait of the city. The few exceptions, for example the elderly man in an Auckland jewellery shop on page 8, merely prove the rule. To people who live in Wellington, much of the cityscape and many of the individuals in it will be familiar. But even to those not on intimate terms with the city and its streets, this portfolio's coherence will be obvious, as well as consistent with Black's previous work – though at once extended here through his deployment of digital technology; and concentrated within the space of a single location. The strategies of close, quirkily detailed observation combined with rapid narrative movement were apparent in his early black and white photographs.

Now, in eighty-two brilliant, disturbing, and compassionate photographs, extended as if across the time it takes for a baby to wake up and recognise the grandfather who is waiting with the child to cross a busy, dangerous street, Peter Black has composed one of the great photo-portraits of our time. A digital *flâneur* on high alert criss-crossing the complex urban landscape, Black has seen and loved the tender, sad, and often humorous details of life lived moment by moment on the streets of his home city.

1 Taranaki St, Wellington, 2009
2 Lambton Quay, Wellington, 2009
3 Taranaki St, Wellington, 2009
4 Lambton Quay, Wellington, 2010
5 Lambton Quay, Wellington, 2010
6 Lambton Quay, Wellington, 2009
7 Lambton Quay, Wellington, 2009
8 Queen St, Auckland, 2009
9 Lambton Quay, Wellington, 2009
10 Queen St, Auckland, 2009
11 Willis St, Wellington, 2009
12 Nairn St, Wellington, 2010
13 Nairn St, Wellington, 2010
14 Farish St, Wellington, 2009
15 Courtney Place, Wellington, 2010
16 Cuba St, Wellington, 2009
17 Lambton Quay, Wellington, 2009
18 Farish St, Wellington, 2009
19 Farish St, Wellington, 2009
20 Willis St, Wellington, 2009
21 Lambton Quay, Wellington, 2009
22 Lambton Quay, Wellington, 2009
23 Lambton Quay, Wellington, 2009
24 Lambton Quay, Wellington, 2009
25 Courtenay Place, Wellington, 2010
26 Nairn St, Wellington, 2010
27 Cuba Mall, Wellington, 2010
28 Nairn St, Wellington, 2009
29 Taranaki St, Wellington, 2009
30 Lambton Quay, Wellington, 2009
31 Waring Taylor St, Wellington, 2009
32 Cuba St, Wellington, 2010
33 Cuba St, Wellington, 2010
34 Ghuznee St, Wellington, 2009
35 Victoria St, Wellington, 2009
36 Lambton Quay, Wellington, 2009
37 Vivian St, Wellington, 2009
38 Cuba Mall, Wellington, 2009
39 Manners Mall, Wellington, 2010
40 Manners Mall, Wellington, 2009
41 Lambton Quay, Wellington, 2009
42 Vivian St, Wellington, 2009
43 Cuba St, Wellington, 2009
44 Manners St, Wellington, 2009
45 Lambton Quay, Wellington, 2009
46 Lambton Quay, Wellington, 2010
47 Cuba St, Wellington, 2009
48 Willis St, Wellington, 2009
49 Lambton Quay, Wellington, 2009
50 Cuba Mall, Wellington, 2009
51 Manners St, Wellington, 2009
52 Cuba Mall, Wellington, 2009
53 Cuba Mall, Wellington, 2009
54 Manners Mall, Wellington, 2008
55 Cuba St, Wellington, 2009
56 Lambton Quay, Wellington, 2009
57 Manners Mall, Wellington, 2009
58 Panama St, Wellington, 2009
59 Manners St, Wellington, 2010
60 Cuba Mall, Wellington , 2010
61 Cuba Mall, Wellington, 2010
62 Cuba Mall, Wellington, 2009
63 Manners Mall, Wellington, 2009
64 Lambton Quay, Wellington, 2009
65 Lambton Quay, Wellington, 2009
66 Cuba St, Wellington, 2009
67 Cuba Mall, Wellington, 2009
68 Cuba St, Wellington, 2010
69 Panama St, Wellington, 2009
70 Courtenay Place, Wellington, 2009
71 Cuba Mall, Wellington, 2009
72 Willis St, Wellington, 2009
73 Cuba Mall, Wellington, 2009
74 Victoria St, Wellington, 2009
75 Lambton Quay, Wellington, 2009
76 Webb St, Wellington, 2009
77 Courtenay Place, Wellington, 2009
78 Sturdee St, Wellington, 2009
79 Cuba Mall, Wellington, 2009
80 Brooklyn Rd, Wellington, 2009
81 Cuba Mall, Wellington, 2010
82 Taranaki St, Wellington, 2009

Selected Exhibitions

2010 *At Home*, Photospace Gallery, Wellington
2009 *New Colour*, Photospace Gallery, Wellington
2008 *Outskirts*, McNamara Gallery, Wanganui
2007 *Flowers and Foliage* (with Robert Mapplethorpe), Te Papa
2007 *Public*, Photospace Gallery, Wellington
2005 *Public*, McNamara Gallery, Wanganui
2003 *Real Fiction*, survey show, City Gallery, Wellington
2002 *Moving Pictures*, McNamara Gallery, Wanganui
1997 *Picture Stories* (with Mary Macpherson), New Work Gallery, Wellington
1995 *Sign Language* (with Mary Macpherson & Lucien Rizos), New Work Gallery, Wellington
1992 *Vox Humana* (with music by Jack Body), Goethe Institute, Wellington
1992 *Sites*, National Library Gallery, Wellington
1990 *Moving Pictures*, City Gallery Wellington
1988 *Foliage*, National Art Gallery, Wellington
1987 *2 Brooklyn Terrace* (commissioned by Peter McLeavey), Exposures Gallery
1986 *Foliage*, New Vision Gallery, Auckland
1986 *Petone Portraits*, Settlers Museum, Petone
1985 *Dancing in the Streets*, City Gallery, Wellington
1984 *Made in New Zealand*, colour photographs, Exposures Gallery, Wellington
1982 *Fifty Photographs*, National Art Gallery, Wellington
1981 *Recent Photographs*, City Gallery Wellington
1981 *New Photos*, Waikato Art Museum, Hamilton
1979 *Photographs by Peter Black*, PhotoForum Gallery, Wellington

Selected Bibliography

Individual titles

2003 *Real Fiction* (Wellington: *Sport* 30)
1998 *Bonjour La France*. Boxed set of photographs (Wellington: Peter Black)
1995 *white horse black dog* (Wellington: *Sport* 15)
1990 *Moving Pictures*. Catalogue (Wellington: Wellington City Art Gallery)
1982 *Fifty Photographs*. Catalogue (Wellington: National Art Gallery)

Group titles

2010 *New Zealand Art from Cook to Contemporary* (Wellington: Te Papa Press)
2009 *Art at Te Papa* (Wellington: Te Papa Press)
2007 *Into the Light – A history of New Zealand Photographs* (Nelson: Craig Potton Publishing)
2006 *Contemporary New Zealand Photographers* (Auckland: Mountain View Publishing)
2006 *'We set out one morning' – Works from the BNZ collection* (Wellington: Private Bank)
2004 *Welcome to the South Seas* (Auckland: AUP)
1999 *Photography and Paradox* (Wellington: NZ Centre for Photography)
1998 *New Zealand, a Century of Images* (Wellington: Te Papa Press)
1993 *New Zealand Photography from the 1840s to the Present* (Auckland: PhotoForum)
1992 *Sites*. Catalogue (Wellington: National Library)
1987 *Politics and Photography* (Wellington: National Art Gallery)
1981 *The Tour* (Wellington: Athol McCredie/Lothians)

Biography

Born in Christchurch in 1948, Peter Black trained with William Main at Wellington Polytechnic, graduating in 1975, and had his first exhibition at PhotoForum in Wellington in 1979. His *Fifty Photographs* at the National Art Gallery in 1982 was the first solo exhibition by a contemporary New Zealand photographer there, during a time when the gallery's Director, Luit Bieringa, took a special interest in New Zealand and international photography.

Since then, Black has had in excess of twenty solo and a similar number of group exhibitions. He was President of PhotoForum (Wellington) in 1980 and a member of the ICON Photographic Collective in 1981. He has received numerous Creative New Zealand grants, and was Artist in Residence at the School of Fine Arts, Canterbury University, in 1993. His work is held in major collections in New Zealand and internationally, including The Museum of New Zealand Te Papa Tongarewa, Auckland Art Gallery, and the National Library Gallery. His photographs have been published and written about in many individual and group publications since the National Art Gallery's 1982 catalogue *Fifty Photographs*, most recently in *Real Fiction* (*Sport* 30, 2003).

Black lives in Wellington with his partner, the photographer and poet Mary Macpherson, with whom he has exhibited jointly on projects including *Picture Stories* (1997) and *Sign Language* (1995, with Lucien Rizos), both at New Work Gallery, Wellington.

I loved you the moment I saw you is Black's fourth and most comprehensive colour portfolio.

Acknowledgements

When I was photographing for this project a street person came up to me and said, 'I've been watching you for weeks, I know what you're trying to do – put me in the book.' I said that a photographic book of this subject matter was a rare thing in New Zealand. Little moments like these give you the courage to continue.

The recession was happening in a big way and I thought that a series about all people, the young, elderly, the well off and the poor could serve as a microcosm of all New Zealand. James (Rangi) seemed to spend most of his time alone, crying quietly to himself. James you are on page 79.

A book like this, of course, takes the goodwill and skills of many people. First, I want to thank Fergus Barrowman of VUP who understood the photographs immediately and is one of the heroes of photographic publishing in New Zealand. Ian Wedde has project managed the book and fund raising from the start. The book would not have been the same without his care and intelligence. Special mention should also be made of James Gilberd (www.photospacegallery.com) for his help in finding contributors, his unwavering support over the years and for responding to the new work with enthusiasm. Also Spencer Levine for his care and attention and designing those details that only a great designer can do.

Thank you is not enough for Luit and Jan Bieringa, Gary Blackman, Peter McLeavey, Anne Noble, Adam Shelton, and Alan Wylde whose leaps of faith made this book possible.

And finally thanks to Mary Macpherson whose photographs taught me that colour photography can have the power of black and white, while at the same time describing more. For Mary – I.L.Y.T.M.I.S.Y.

I Loved You The Moment I Saw You
Peter Black

First published in New Zealand in 2011 by
Victoria University Press

TE WHARE WĀNANGA O TE ŪPOKO O TE IKA A MĀUI
VICTORIA
UNIVERSITY OF WELLINGTON

Victoria University of Wellington
PO Box 600, Wellington, New Zealand
http://www.victoria.ac.nz/vup

Design by Spencer Levine
Printed by 1010 Printing International Ltd

This book has been generously supported by
Luit and Jan Bieringa
Gary Blackman
Peter McLeavey
Anne Noble
Adam Shelton
Alan Wylde

This book has been typeset using Stag by Christian Schwartz and printed on 160gsm Gold East matt art paper.

National Library of New Zealand
Cataloguing-in-Publication Data

Black, Peter, 1948-
I loved you the moment I saw you
/ Peter Black.
ISBN 978-0-86473-659-8
1. Photography—New Zealand—
Wellington. I. Title.
770.99363—dc 22